Coaching
the Full Court
Man-to-Man Press

Burrall Paye

Parker Publishing Co., Inc.
West Nyack, New York

Library of Congress Cataloging in Publication Data

Paye, Burrall
  Coaching the full court man-to-man press.

  Includes index.
    1. Basketball coaching. 2. Basketball--Defense.
I. Title.
GV885.3.P38   796.32'307'7   78-3831
ISBN 0-13-139063-5

Printed in the United States of America

To

All the coaches, players, and friends who
gave their knowledge freely, especially my
brother, Waford, who gave the most.

How This Book Will Help You Develop the Man Press

This book is a complete guide to the full court man-to-man presses. It is also a finger-tip reference to cure certain segments of your defense.

Each section develops its ideas completely. That fact will enable you to confine your research to only that section. You will not have to waste time during the busy winter months flipping pages, using the index, or checking the table of contents. Merely re-read the desired material. Each installment comprises an entity in itself.

For example, traps and switches make up Chapter 2. All traps—blitz trap, jump trap, run and jump trap, long run and jump trap, jumping out and showing, hedging-then-trapping, give-outside-then-take-it-away trap—have received extensive coverage. The same thing holds true for switching and all its related fundamental discussions. Diagrams describe in lucid detail each team stunt as well as each individual drill.

Fully defined individual fundamentals, complete and succinct, occupy the early part of the book. Stunts that force the offense to perform as the defense dictates follow in rapid-fire order. Strategies of each of the defensive ideas comprise another portion of the book. Sections on methods to force the five-second violation, schemes to halt the advancement of the ball, and programs of action to compel the attackers to the area of the court where the defense wants them give new ideas as well as confirm old ones about two-, three-, four-, and five-man fundamental defensive attacks.

All of the acceptable full court team man-to-man defenses, such as the run and jump press, receive extensive coverage. Even if you do not wish to press with the man-to-man, you can use the pressure tactics described in Chapters 1 through 5 to improve your favorite zone press. The text can even acquaint the offensive-minded coach with methods of attacking the oldest and safest press in basketball.

The area man-to-man press, destined to become a staple in defensive basketball and described in detail in this book, grants all the conservative protection of the man-to-man press and provides for all the chaotic trapping conditions that the zone presses conjure up.

Couple the above arguments with the various methods of forcing errors, of dictating offensive maneuvers, of disrupting offensive game plans, and a team has a championship full court pressure defense.

Keeping defensive pressure on opponents from opening tip to final buzzer will disrupt their timing, confuse their attack, and destroy their mental poise while tiring them physically. If this pressure does not result in easy shots, then applying the press does not hurt the defending team. Anything gained from the defensive squeeze, therefore, must help the defense win the game.

Unlike the zone presses, the man-to-man presses will seldom, if ever, concede the uncontested lay-up. That fact alone will permit teams to use the man-to-man presses for the entire season, gaining what they can gain from them, without fear of being beaten by them.

Burrall Paye

Contents

Talking: Back Line to Front Line · Developing Anticipation · Developing Quickness · Developing Aggressiveness · Busy Hands · Busy Eyes · Footwork and Stance · Challenging the Ball Handler · Harassment of the Dribbler · How and When to Draw the Charge · When and How to Flick · Force Dribbler to Weak Hand · Individual Attacking Techniques Analyzed and Defended · Recovering When Passed Up by a Dribbler · Spacing · Playing the First Pass Receiver · Playing the Second Pass Receiver · Playing the Third Pass Receiver · Playing the Fourth Pass Receiver · Recovering When Passed Up by a Pass · How to Pick Up the Loose Man · Watch Floor Position · How to Teach Players to Analyze and React · A Denial Pressure and Passing Lane Drill

Hedging · Floating · Double-Teaming · The Loose Trap and the Tight Trap · Responsibility of the Container · Responsibility of the Trapper · Trap After Loss of Dribble · Trap Before Loss of Dribble · Best Time to Trap · Best Areas of Court for Trapping · How to Recognize and Cover Passing Lanes · Jump

2 Coaching Different Methods of Trapping and Switching *(continued)*

Trap · Jumping Out and Showing · Hedging Followed by a Trap · Blitz Trap · Run and Jump Trap · Long Run and Jump Trap · Give the Outside, Then Take It Away · Summary of Traps · Double-Teaming and Shooting the Gaps · How to Switch Out of an Unsuccessful Trap · How to Switch · Jump Switch · Blitz Switch · Run and Jump Switch · Long Run and Jump Switch · Summary of Switches · A Rotation Drill to Determine Who Switches to Whom · Run and No-Jump Strategy

3 Preventing the In-Bounds Pass   85

Playing the Out-of-Bounds Passer · Double on the Out-of-Bounds Passer · Make Weak Ball Handlers Handle the Ball · Playing the In-Bounds Receiver · Face-Guard · Denial · The Center Field · The Short Stop · The Left Field · Analyzing and Defending Different Methods of In-Bounding the Ball

4 Strategies for Stopping Advancement of the Ball   113

Force Change of Direction · Give the Outside, Then Take It Away · Stealing the Pass · Fan · Funnel · Fan or Funnel (Let the Offense Call It) · Coming out of Double-Teams · Traps and Switching · Run and Jumps · Best Areas to Double-Team · A Rotation Drill to Stop an Escaped Dribbler's Advancement

5 Principles of the Man-to-Man Full Court Press   125

Deny All Penetration to the Middle Lane · Deny All Vertical Passes · Double-Team All Player and Ball Crossings · Float on Players More than One Pass Away · Keep Proper Spacing · Every Defender Must Be Ahead of the Ball · Physically Float—Mentally

**5 Principles of the Man-to-Man
Full Court Press** *(continued)*

Play Passing Lane · Weakside Defender Stops Drib-
bler · Relocate as Ball Is Passed · Never Give the
Lay-Up · Transition: A Press Drill When You Don't
Score

**6 Strategies for Stunting from
the Full Court Man Press**

Three-Men-and-a-Tandem · Numbering Press ·
Dropping and Delaying · Baiting the Dribbler ·
Show and Tell · Two-on-Two Stunts · Three-on-
Three Stunts · Four-on-Four Stunts

7 Employing the Run and Jump Press

Major Principles of the Run and Jump · Drills to
Teach the Run and Jump · Responsibilities of the
Container · Responsibilities of the Trapper · Duties
of the Gap Shooter · Duties of the React Man ·
Duties of the Goalie · Plays Involving the Run and
Jump · Attacking the Reverse Dribble · Attacking the
Clearout · Attacking the Long Pass Offense · Attack-
ing with One Gap Shooter · Attacking with a Gap
Shooter and a React Man · Attacking with a Full Rota-
tion

8 Coaching the Area Man-to-Man Press

Rules of the Area Man-to-Man Press · Placement of
Personnel · Giving the Zone Look · Rotating from a
2-2-1 to a 1-2-1-1 Look · Rotating from a 1-2-1-1 to a
2-2-1 Look · The Forty Series · The Thirty Series ·
The Twenty Series · The Ten Series

**9 Defensing the Best Known Methods
of Attacking the Man Press**

Flashing and Posting · Sideline Type Offenses · Middle Lane Offenses · Short Pass Game · Long Pass

**9   Defensing the Best Known Methods
     of Attacking the Man Press (continued)**

Game · Dribble and Split Game · Patterned Offenses
· The Virginia Box · The One-Man Attack: The
Clearout · The 2 Down-3 Back Attack · The 3
Down-2 Back Attack · The 4 Down-1 Back Attack ·
The 5 Down-0 Back Attack · Summary

Philosophy · Match-Ups · Have Two Plans · Pre-
Season Practices to Develop Pressure Players · Pre-
Game Practices to Develop a Game Plan · Game Ad-
justments to Make Press Work Better · Game-to-
Game Adjustments · Coaches Must Also Analyze and
React

Coaching
the Full Court
Man-to-Man Press

1

Developing Individual Pressing Tactics

Full court pressing coaches must design their defenses to last for a full game, a complete season, a career. Defensive teams can hide a few weak defenders, but they cannot conceal them for long periods of time. A coach must either develop those weak defenders into better defensive performers or abandon his hopes of pressing an entire game.

Strong defenders improve with proper instruction, and weak defenders, under such schooling, advance more rapidly than the strong. Fundamental savvy and hard work refine the strong and rectify the weak. Correct practice meliorates the individual; incorrect practice prolongs, often postpones, his development.

Regardless of where your defenders now stand on the scale of individual cultivation, after you read this chapter your team's quality of play will increase immeasureably. The weakest individual defender will reach the previous level of the strongest, and the strongest will get even better.

TALKING: BACK LINE TO FRONT LINE

For a pressing team to achieve its highest degree of success, the back line must communicate to the front line. The back line has full view of the court while the front line sees only those players who bring the ball down the court. The back line calls the stunts that you have not signalled.

Talking, therefore, becomes a prerequisite to successful pressing. Drills will implant the required methods into the players. Talking, like all defensive fundamentals, can be infused by repetitious drilling.

Procedure (Diagram 1-1):

1. Line all players up on the end line.
2. First player in line races backward to the 28-foot line where he pivots facing out-of-bounds. He defensively slides to the free throw line extended (left sideline), hitting the palms of his hands on the floor with each slide. He again pivots facing midcourt and defensively slides to the opposite (right) sideline, then races backward to the point where the left sideline intersects the midcourt line. He slides across the midcourt line telling his

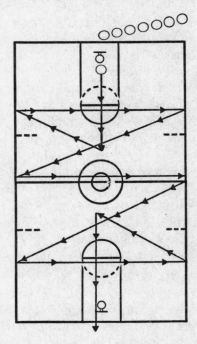

Diagram 1-1

teammates what he sees in front of him, helping them avoid pileups. When he reaches the right sideline at midcourt, he races backward to the free throw line extended on the left sideline. He pivots, facing the end line, and slides defensively to the right sideline. When he touches the right sideline, he pivots, looking inward, and slides up to the 28-foot mark. From there, he races backward to the end line. While racing through this maze, he constantly crosses the paths of his teammates. Both he and his teammates have their backs to each other. Only through talking will they circumvent contact. Defensive players should touch the palms of their hands on the floor with every defensive slide. They should accomplish this without bobbing their heads.

3. Second player in the line begins racing backward when the first player reaches the first free throw line.
4. A trip downfloor and back by each player takes less than a minute. You can require one or more trips.

Objectives:

1. To teach communication.
2. To teach defensive sliding, staying low without bobbing heads.
3. To condition legs for pressing an entire game.

DEVELOPING ANTICIPATION

Time remaining, our opponent's ability and the score help us determine the amount of gambling allowed, the degree of anticipation. Physically float—mentally play passing lane (Chapter 5), a principle of full court man-to-man pressing, demands anticipation.

Watching the eyes and the feet of the passer will cue the anticipator to the direction of the pass. Quick footwork will get the passing lane covered and produce the interception.

Under great duress, such as a double-team, a passer will usually look directly toward his intended receiver. His feet will point in the direction of the pass. When the feet are parallel, expect a short bounce or chest pass. Staggered feet usually indicate a longer pass; for example, the baseball pass or the two-handed overhead pass. A step to the side or a leap into the air can produce either a short or a long pass. However, the success of such a pass diminishes in direct proportion to its intended length.

Later in this chapter, in the section on Spacing, we will offer a drill which not only develops full court anticipation but demands proper spacing.

DEVELOPING QUICKNESS

Strength improves quickness. Many textbooks and independent companies have easily assessable strength development programs. You can pick the course best suited for your intentions and needs.

Coaches can conduct drills that will increase quickness of both the feet and the hands. Holding an object between the hands and dropping it as the hands clap together to stop its fall helps develop hand quickness. Forcing the balls of the feet to rise ever so slightly off the floor increases foot movement. Drills requiring quick turning of the feet speed development of the feet. Ball-handling drills that impel concerted foot and hand movement help. Another drill: one player faces a wall about three feet from it. A teammate stands behind him and tosses the ball hard off the wall. The defender facing the wall must recover the ball before it hits the floor.

DEVELOPING AGGRESSIVENESS

Aggressiveness, the very essence of pressing, increases with progressive drills and proper emphasis. Attacking, never retreating, should be stressed. Even as the offense advances down the floor, the coach should tell his defenders not to retreat farther than the point of the ball. At that point the defense should attack again. Such mental aggressiveness must be demanded. Mental aggressiveness comes before physical aggressiveness.

To develop physical aggressiveness, we divide our players into two lines, one at each of the points of intersection of the free throw lane with the baseline. A coach stands directly under the basket, and he rolls, bounces, or tosses the ball in all directions. As the ball leaves the coach's hand, the front players in each line contest for the elusive ball. The retriever plays offense while the other player defends in a one-on-one contest.

A coach can alter the beginning position and compel greater aggressiveness. For example, the lines can be formed at alternate corners of the court, and the ball can be rolled down the midcourt line or from one neutral corner toward the other.

One of our favorite aggressive drills involves all five first teamers. Three players act as rebounders while two will fight for possession of the tip. The tipper stays under the basket while the other two rebounders must race to the opposite baseline and back. The two retrievers of the tip contest each other for the ball in the free throw circle. The player who gains possession plays the loser in a one-on-one contest. But that player must score prior to the arrival of the two men who ran to the opposite baseline, or he will face a one-against-three situation.

BUSY HANDS

Hands must constantly jab at a dribbler, like the strikes of a snake. They must frantically wave in a windmill fashion around the player who has lost his dribble. And they must forever be present in the passing lane to the first pass receiver, discouraging any attempt to pass directly downcourt.

By jabbing at the dribbler, we hope to stop the dribble. By the windmill waving, we hope to obstruct the passer's view and maybe deflect his pass. By having a hand in the immediate passing lanes, we intend to steal any babied bounce, chest, or lob pass.

BUSY EYES

Pressure defense demands that all defenders be above the advancement of the ball. Each of those defenders must see all that happens in front of them and as much as they can of the floor behind them. They must also be told what goes on behind them. Each player must assess his position and make a proper judgment based on his calculations. The more he sees, the better the information he receives and the better and the quicker he can make a logical decision.

Eyes, therefore, play an important part in the man-to-man full court pressure defense. Watching the eyes of the passer indicates where he will consider throwing the ball. Watching the passer's feet tells how far he will throw it. A ball held over the head by two hands can only be passed, and probably at a great distance. Using proper stances and a swivel-head, the defender can determine how players are moving outside his peripheral view; and the defender can maintain a proper positioning on his own man as well as a helping position to his teammates.

When the ball moves, when the attacker with the ball moves, or when the defender's man drifts, the defender must move. He must reassess his position, and he must reachieve proper coverage. His stance, swivel-head, and peripheral vision should instantly alert him to all of this movement.

FOOTWORK AND STANCE

Different positions require different stances. Each stance will be discussed thoroughly in the section on that particular position.

The intention of the team defense determines to a large degree the stance used on the dribbler. If we try to steal the dribble, flick the ball away, or cut the dribbler toward help, we will use a staggered stance and overplay. If we want to contain the dribbler, we play parallel with nose-on-the-ball techniques. The first pass receiver in either of the passing lanes, unless they are more than 20 feet away from the passer, will be played with a closed denial stance. Receivers more than 20 feet away, like attackers who have an offensive man between them and the ball, are played with an open stance, physically playing the men but mentally playing the passing lane. The open stance offers a better chance to intercept, a better opportunity to help; the closed stance forbids a pass.

After developing anticipation, quickness, aggressiveness, talking, busy hands, busy eyes, and proper stances, a defender reaches the stage where he can adequately challenge the ball handler.

CHALLENGING THE BALL HANDLER

Constant pressure exerted on the dribbler prevents him from making accurate passes. Compelling the dribbler to stop his dribble and to pass the ball becomes a cornerstone of pressure man-to-man defense.

To accomplish this objective, we offer fundamental drills for the individual, two men, three men, and four men before advancing to the full concerted team motion. How and where we challenge the ball handler depends upon the stunt we have invoked.

Ball handlers must experience pressure from opening tip to final buzzer. Many times, one bad pass leads to another and another. Often, before the opposition can regroup, rigor mortis has set in.

If we defend the dribbler one-on-one, we expect to force a change of direction three times before he can reach front court. If we defend the dribbler team-wise, we intend to impel three passes before he can arrive at a set-up point. We have methods to steal the dribble; we have team techniques to steal the pass. Yet our retreat and rotation techniques will deny the easy shot.

HARASSMENT OF THE DRIBBLER

Stopping the dribble helps the team defense almost as much as stealing the dribble. When the dribbler picks up the ball, we immediately attempt to pick off the pass. But first, let's steal the dribble.

Trail hands are expected to steal crossover dribbles. Reverse dribbles, unless handled properly by the same hand, are easy prey for the steal and the wide open driving lay-up. Reverse dribbles can be flicked away. Behind-the-back dribbles can become walking violations. All three offensive moves can result in charging when played properly by the defense. Each defensive technique of each offensive maneuver has a section in this chapter devoted to it. Developmental drills accompany explanations.

Modern players will not pick up their dribble when defensed by only one man. Two or more defenders can compel the dribbler to pass. One defender can channel the dribbler, by means of an overplay, to an area of the court desired by the defense. While in that area, the defense can hedge, trap, double-team, jump trap, blitz trap, run and jump trap, switch, jump switch, blitz switch, run and jump switch, and jump out and show. These defensive moves, when used discreetly, should force the dribbler to pick up the ball. Only a pass could continue the offense. Each of these defensive techniques have sections devoted to them in Chapter 2. Developmental drills again accompany explanations.

Mixing team techniques with individual defensive maneuvers confuses and harasses the best dribbler. Combine these with the one-on-one containment and dribble-used drill (see next to last section in this chapter) to complete the devastation of teams that want to dribble the ball downcourt against the man-to-man full court pressure defense.

HOW AND WHEN TO DRAW THE CHARGE

Defenders can draw the charge from a dribbler, a cutter, or a pass receiver. Basketball rules require different defensive body positioning for each.

Defenders do not have to give a dribbler an inch. Contact by the attacker received by the defender in the torso demands a charging call, regardless of the position of the feet. The attacker must get his head and shoulder in front of the defender for a blocking call.

But an attacker without the ball, a cutter, must be allowed a step to change his direction. A defender who has established both feet on the floor prior to contact in the torso has given the cutter the required step.

A pass receiver who cuts with his head facing away from his defender and toward the passer has a right to the area of the floor where the pass leads. So does the defender. Referees will judge blocking or charging on one question: Did the attacker have time to change direction if he had known the defender was there? Defenders, therefore, should have both feet firmly on the floor and at least three feet from the pass receiver. Often, defenders who do not draw the charge force the receiver to walk.

In our presses, defenders must approach the point of reception before the ball and the receiver arrive. Not only does this permit us to draw the charge or perpetrate the walk, but we can force a momentary delay by the new pass receiver. Before he can dribble or find another pass receiver, the defender's teammates should have had time to recover to their new positions. Defensive coaches must demand this coverage by their defenders, benching those who operate delinquently or tardily.

To protect the defender who draws the charge from injury, have him put both arms in front of his body, one at waist level and the other at chest level. The defender should be on the balls of his feet, patting the floor. At the exact moment of contact, he should push backward off the balls of his feet, letting his legs fly out. He should land on his buttocks about three feet from the foul. He should raise his top leg in a semi-bent position as he rolls on his side. This prevents injury if a big man falls on a small guard. Pressure teams must master this technique to prevent injuries during practice as well as during games. Drills must accompany all three defensive methods.

The zig-zag drills, explained later in this chapter, provide training for drawing the charge off the dribbler. A three-on-three drill gives defenders practice at drawing the charge off a cutter and a pass receiver. As the team defense develops, this three-on-three skeleton becomes more evident.

Procedure (Diagram 1-2):

1. Line players up as shown. Go downfloor and back before rotating positions. Rotate from 1 to X1 to 2 to X2 and 3 to X3 to the end of the line. Next player in line becomes 1.
2. 1 has ball and must pass to 2. If 2 breaks toward passer, 1, X2 draws the charge, illustrating drawing the charge on a cutter.
3. If 2 likes, he may race downfloor for a baseball pass. X3 would then attempt to draw a charge on the looking-backward pass receiver. X2 would have to switch to 3. If

X3 could not draw the charge, he would force the violation or slow down the next pass.

4. X1 would play the passer, trying to force the bad or
   hurried pass.
5. If 1 passes to 2, 1 exchanges responsibilities with 2 (as
   shown in Diagram 1-2). X1 tries to draw the charge on
   the cutting 1. X3 tries to draw the charge as 2 throws the
   long lob or baseball pass. X3 and X1 would exchange
   men. X2 would try to force 2 to throw an errant pass.
6. 2, in the beginning, cannot dribble after receiving a pass
   from 1. After learning the run and jump drills, 2 can
   dribble or pass.

Objectives:

1. To teach defending the out-of-bounds passer.
2. To teach defending the in-bounds receiver.
3. To teach drawing the charge on a cutter; drawing the
   charge and forcing a violation on a downcourt receiver.
4. To teaching switching when passed up by a pass.
5. To teach passing and receiving offensively.

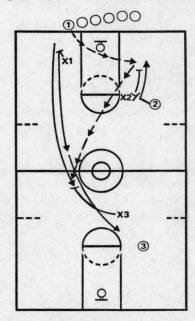

Diagram 1-2

WHEN AND HOW TO FLICK

Flicking is a dangerous individual defensive maneuver, often judged a foul. But when viewed in the defensive team concept, it can help destroy an offense. When the defender misses the flick, the dribbling attacker gains a momentary numerical advantage. Defensive players must recover quickly, and a team switching technique becomes mandatory.

To successfully flick, the defender must force the reverse (Diagram 1-3). As the attacker reverses, the defender steps directly behind the heel of the attacker's pivot foot. This step should be an exaggerated stretch. His body should stretch and he should extend his arm to its fullest length. He should then tap the ball to a teammate. If he misses the flick, he should continue in the direction his body is going as he switches defensive assignments with a teammate.

A later section, Playing the Dribbler Individually, contains a flicking drill. Many team defenses, described throughout the book, include the flicking techniques. Each team defense and each individual technique will be described completely and succinctly in the chapters on team defense.

Flicking works best against the reverse dribble. But flicking can occur against any change of direction dribble or when a defender slips up behind a dribbler. It can also occur in team strategies: for example, give the outside, then take it away.

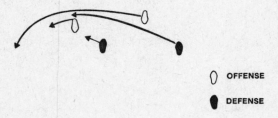

○ OFFENSE

● DEFENSE

Diagram 1-3

FORCE DRIBBLER TO WEAK HAND

All players have a weak hand. Although good dribblers work hard to train their weak hand, one hand will invariably be stronger than the other.

The weak hand may change with the maneuver used. Most attackers reverse dribble best going right, reversing left; so the defense would prefer to force the dribbler left, overplay and compel the reverse dribble right. Usually, players can crossover dribble with equal proficiency; but behind-the-back dribblers have favorite sides. Most often, the favorite side involves taking the ball behind the back with the right hand.

Defensive coaches should consider the immediate move that follows the execution of the basic three dribbles: reverse, crossover, and behind the back. Behind-the-back and reverse dribblers, more often than not, cannot change directions immediately after executing those techniques. They require another step or two before they can recover and adjust. A defender in the path of such a dribbler could force a violation or draw a charge. This would constitute the weak side of such a dribbler.

Turning dribblers toward their weak hand enables team stunts to work better. It not only constrains the passer to his weakest point, delaying the start of the team attack, but also tips the remaining defenders to act in concert, giving them a better opportunity to intercept. Two- and three-men stunts also operate more efficiently from the weak hand.

Coaches may key their stunts to commence with the turn to the weak hand, with the turn to either hand, with a dribble toward a teammate, with the arrival at a certain area, or with any pre-arranged signal. But when we desperately need the ball, we prefer the weak-hand omen.

INDIVIDUAL ATTACKING TECHNIQUES
ANALYZED AND DEFENDED

Man-to-man pressure defense consists of three basic strategies: containment, channeling the dribbler to a trap, and defensing the dribbler individually. Each has a place in the team defense; and when used interchangeably, they can keep the best offenses guessing, confused, and off-balance. The bench can call the strategy, or the coach can allow the defenders to analyze and react to one another.

Containment

When we contain, we want nose-to-nose defense. After channelling a dribbler by an overplay, either to steal the ball himself or to drive the dribbler toward a trap, the attacker has tendencies to hurry against containment. That haste results in offensive mistakes.

While being contained, the dribbler worries. When will the trap occur? When will the defender try to steal the dribble, draw the charge, or flick the ball to a teammate? These become questions in the minds of the best ball handler. Such queries force the attacker to hurry, to make mistakes against the slow containment. Often, an attacker will charge a defender by trying to hurriedly drive past the nose-to-nose container. The nose-to-nose container can easily receive the blow in the torso by half-stepping in front of the hasty driver.

Channelling the Dribbler to the Trap

We have several means of trapping (see Chapter 2), but we drive the dribbler to the trap by an overplay. We overplay the attacker one-half a man (nose of the defender on the ball). The driver cannot continue without charging, so he heads in another direction. The new direction, toward our pre-signalled trap, must be maintained and encouraged by the defender. Once turned, we want the dribbler's defender about three feet in front of a line through the dribbler parallel to the baseline, and we want the nose of the defender on the non-dribbling armpit. This encourages the dribbler to continue his path because there is no resistance. And, it prevents the dribbler from driving by the defender and choosing another path. Because of the relative speed and quickness of the defender and the ball handler, there are occasions when three feet are not enough. On those occasions, the defender must judge wisely and react accurately.

Defensing the Dribbler Individually

We also begin individual defensing with an overplay. Defensive overplays demand that attackers find a new avenue of attack. While they look for this new route, the defender attempts an individual maneuver to force a turnover. The attacker can use a reverse dribble, a crossover dribble, or a behind-the-back-dribble. We teach our defenders methods to steal the ball, to flick the ball away, and to draw the charge against each of these offensive counters. Each will be explained in separate sections and drills to develop those techniques will be offered at the conclusion of each discussion.

Stealing the dribble off the reverse. Stealing the dribble himself, flicking the ball to a teammate, and drawing the charge himself represent our individual techniques of forcing violations when facing a reverse dribbler. We also use team stunts, consisting of two or more defenders, to gain a turnover. Explanations of the individual methods appear here; team strategies are presented and explained throughout the book.

Because the dribbler's body stays between the defender and the dribble, the attacker must make a mistake if the defensive man steals the ball. But the same footwork used to steal the ball is used to flick and to draw the charge.

The defender must first overplay, compelling the dribbler to change his direction. That is also the first move to impel the crossover dribble or the behind-the-back dribble. That overplay must be one-half a man.

As the attacker reverses, the defender must step directly behind the heel of the pivot foot (Diagram 1-3). To steal the dribble, the attacker must switch dribbling hands as he pivots. This leaves the ball out where it can be stolen. The hand nearest the pivot foot (the left hand in Diagram 1-3) swipes the ball away from the direction the attacker is headed. A steal should result in a wide open driving lay-up.

Flicking the ball off of the reverse. Excellent dribblers will not switch hands while reversing. They will maintain ball control with one hand (left hand in Diagram 1-3) until they have completed their pivot and have begun dribbling in their new direction.

To flick the ball away the defender stretches his step, his body, and his arm as far as possible. And at the moment when he feels he can reach the ball, the defender slaps the ball in the new direction of the attacker. The defender's teammates should be between their men and the dribbler. A teammate should recover the flick, tossing a lead pass to the flicker who, after successfully flicking, has raced downfloor for the pass and a lay-up.

Drawing the charge off of the reverse. Attackers who have a history of turning back toward their old direction after reversing will commit charges. Defenders should play for this charge. Instead of flicking or stealing, the defender should straighten his upper body (the torso), preparing for the charging blow. Although this defensive maneuver will not get the uncontested lay-up, it will get the turnover.

Flicking and stealing maneuvers are used prior to half-court or in the front court, late in a game that we are losing. This gives the defense the best opportunity to recover.

We also teach a quick four-step method of regaining position after forcing a reverse. We use the four-step method from baseline to baseline.

The four-step method is used to reestablish position after compelling an attacker to reverse, sometimes drawing the charge. It is more conservative and represents containment. The four-step maneuvers are employed when we run and jump, when we are ahead, when the opposition gets the ball over the time line and we are using individual techniques.

After overplaying the dribbler, the defender anticipates the offensive reverse and reacts with the quick four-step which will, on occasions, enable the defender to draw the charge. Diagram 1-4 depicts the four quick steps the defender uses. Those same four steps prevent any advantage an attacker might gain from the behind-the-back move. This expedites teaching, leaving the defense less to learn. When facing the reverse dribble, the torso should be straight, preparing for the hard contact of the charge.

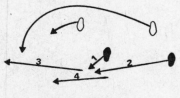

Diagram 1-4

***Developmental drill used to steal, flick, and draw charge
off of the reverse.*** Coaches should begin instructing their defenders by letting the offense walk through the reverse using two
hands (stealing) and then one hand (flicking). Then the coach
should require his defenders to draw the charge from both offensive methods. When first teaching the defense, an attacker begins at the free throw line and uses only the reverse dribble (one
hand or two hands, but not both). The defender uses only one
method. He progresses to using any method the situation calls
for.

Procedure (Diagram 1-5):

1. Put an offensive player and a defender in each line.
2. Limit the attacker to the reverse dribble.
3. Begin by limiting the defender to flicking, to stealing, or
   to drawing the charge.
4. After the coach feels the defender can flick, steal, and
   draw the charge, the coach can insist on the defense
   deciding which technique to use.

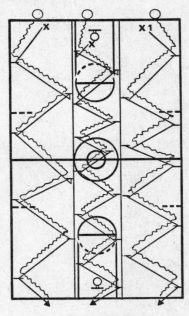

Diagram 1-5

5. After attempting a flick, charge, or steal, successful or not, the ball, the attacker, and the defender return to the spot of the steal, flick, or charge and continue downfloor.
6. Three successful flicks, steals, or charges should occur in one full court trip.
7. Attacker reverses downfloor and back before exchanging places with the defender.

Objectives:

1. To teach flicking, stealing, and drawing the charge off of the reverse.
2. To teach overplaying and recovering for another overplay.
3. To teach proper individual man-to-man pressure defense.
4. To teach the reverse dribble offensively.

Stealing the dribble off of the crossover. Because the ball is unprotected momentarily as the dribbler swings it from one hand to the other in front of his body while executing the crossover, it falls easy prey to the defensive trail hand. The trail hand should be low with the palms facing inward. As the ball leaves one hand directed toward the other, the dribbler usually steps backward. Because of this backward step, the defender should step forward and to the outside with his trail foot. At the same time he should swipe inward with his trail hand.

By stepping outside, the defender can regain overplay positioning should he fail to steal the dribble. His second step in regaining overplay position would require bringing his feet back together. The former lead foot would be brought near the outside stepping trail foot. The former trail foot would explode outside. If these three steps do not place the defender in an overplay, it would at least place him nose-to-nose, and he could begin working for another overplay.

Flicking off of the crossover. To successfully flick when the attacker crossover dribbles, the defender must circle the attacker. This would give the dribbler a straight line drive downfloor. We discourage flicking against the crossover.

However, late in a game which we are losing, a defender will flick the crossover by racing downfloor behind the dribbler while a teammate helps him by hedging (see Chapter 2). This gambling maneuver cannot succeed often. So we use it infrequently and only in desperate situations.

Drawing the charge off of the crossover. The same three-count steps used to steal the dribble are employed to draw the charge. Instead of letting the trail hand swipe at the ball, the defender, who has anticipated the crossover, concentrates fully on reestablishing a new overplay position with his torso straight. Contact there by the attacker constitutes a charge.

Drill used to flick, steal, and draw charge off of crossover. Defenders learn best by progressive drills. During the first few days, let the attackers walk through the crossover while the defenders visualize (by stepping through) their flicking, stealing, and drawing the charge techniques. Coaches can progress their players live by using only a small portion of the court (free throw lane, for example). In this small area the coach can better correct his defender. When the coach feels his defender has progressed satisfactorily, he can move to the full court drill of Diagram 1-5.

Procedure (Diagram 1-5):

1. Put an offensive player and a defender in each lane.
2. Limit the attacker to the crossover dribble.
3. Limit the defender to either flicking (we teach this last), stealing, or drawing the charge.
4. After satisfactory progress, the coach can let the defender decide which technique to use. He can even mix them up on the same trip downfloor.
5. After attempting a steal, flick, or charge, successful or not, the ball, the attacker, and the defender return to the spot of the flick, steal, or charge and continue downfloor.
6. Three successful steals, charges, or flicks should occur in one trip downfloor.
7. Attacker crossover dribbles downfloor and back before exchanging places with the defender.

Objectives:
1. To teach flicking, stealing, and drawing the charge.
2. To teach overplaying and recovering for another overplay.
3. To teach proper individual man-to-man defense.
4. To teach the crossover dribble offensively.

Forcing violations off of the behind-the-back move. Behind-the-back dribbles, clinically speaking, contain the perfect individual mechanism to destroy full court man-to-man presses. This maneuver provides maximum protection of the ball (body between the defender and the ball), and it permits the attacker to keep his complete view of what's happening downcourt. Fortunately for the defense, many offensive coaches have considered the behind-the-back dribble a show-off move and have failed to teach it. But in recent years it has become a popular offensive maneuver.

Stealing the ball is practically impossible. Forcing the violation is easier. Drawing the charge is the best bet. Each defensive maneuver, however, originates with an overplay, followed closely by anticipating the offensive move and establishing a quick four-step into another overplay (Diagram 1-4). By establishing the new overplay position, the dribbler might stop quickly without proper control of the dribble. A quick step forward by the defender's inside trail foot and a swipe by the trail hand might deflect the ball, and could cause the dribbler to lose control. Bellying up with the torso straight could draw the charge.

When the dribbler faces a quick overplay off the behind-the-back move, the attacker will, most likely, either pick up the dribble or immediately go into a crossover or a reverse. If the attacker is blasting full speed and tries to pick up the dribble, he will probably walk or charge. If the dribbler counters with a crossover or a reverse, the defense can immediately steal the new move, flick the ball away, or draw the charge. Most dribblers aid the defense by not practicing the behind-the-back move followed by a reverse or a crossover. Consequently, the counter is easier to steal, to flick, or to draw the charge.

It is hard to flick the ball away from the behind-the-back dribble. Teammates must hedge and we must chase from behind to accomplish this (see section on Flicking the Crossover).

Drill used to force violations off of behind-the-back move. Defenders must drill, drill, drill until their actions and reactions become instinctive. Walking through the behind-the-back dribble and the defense of it enables the defender to better visualize what is expected of him. Using a small area of the court, the free throw lane, permits the coach to see and to correct the defensive mistakes. Then, progressing to a live full court drill (Diagram 1-5) instills confidence (using only one-third of the court) in the defender while permitting more overplays.

Procedure (Diagram 1-5):

1. Put an offensive player and a defender in each lane.
2. Limit the attacker to the behind-the-back dribble.
3. Limit the defender to either flicking, stealing, or drawing the charge.
4. After satisfactory progress, the coach can let the defender decide which technique to use. He can even mix them up on the same trip downfloor.
5. After attempting a steal, a flick, or a charge, successful or not, the ball, the attacker, and the defender return to the spot of the flick, steal, or charge and continue downfloor.
6. Three successful steals, charges, or flicks should occur in one trip downfloor.
7. Attacker dribbles behind-the-back downfloor and back before exchanging places with the defender.

Objectives:

1. To teach flicking, stealing, and drawing the charge.
2. To teach overplaying and recovering for another overplay.
3. To teach proper individual man-to-man defense.
4. To teach the crossover, reverse, and especially the behind-the-back dribble (see statement below).

After a few days of behind-the-back dribbling only, let the dribbler use a combination of moves following the behind-the-back dribble. Do not permit a dribble between the behind-the-back and either the reverse or the crossover.

Combinations. After successfully defending the reverse, the crossover, and the behind-the-back, we begin encouraging combinations. We teach doubles and triples. Doubles would consist of a reverse followed by a crossover, a reverse followed by a behind-the-back, etc. Triples, for example, would mix the reverse, the crossover, then the reverse again in rapid order. Doubles require two quick defensive overplays; triples must have three quick overplays. Teaching combinations helps the offense become better ball handlers, and it aids the defense in stopping the great ball handlers.

Another type of combination that we encourage mixes containment, channelling the dribbler to a trap, and defensing a dribbler individually. Chapter 2 offers more about these combination prototypes.

Zig-zag drill. We introduce the zig-zag drill after the defenders have mastered defense of the reverse, the crossover, the behind-the-back dribble, and the combinations. The attacker in the zig-zag drill can decide how he wants to attack. The defender must dictate to the dribbler what he will allow and then the defender must stop that dictate.

Procedure (Diagram 1-5):
1. Line players up as shown: one attacker, one defender.
2. The offense advances the ball.
3. The defense races back and turns the offense by means of an overplay.
4. We start the season without using the hands, progressing into hand use after footwork is mastered.
5. We encourage defense to cut man off at least three times in each half-court.
6. Offense attacks downcourt and back before exchanging positions with the defender.

Objectives:
1. To teach cut-offs by an overplay.
2. To teach individual pressure defense over the full court.
3. To condition.

4. To teach advancing ball offensively under pressure.
5. To teach offense and defense of reverse, crossover, behind-the-back, and combination dribbling.

RECOVERING WHEN PASSED UP BY A DRIBBLER

Regardless of how well taught the defense is, or how well the defense executes, the time comes, during almost all games, when a defender gets passed up by a dribbler, making it momentarily impossible for that defender to adhere to the basic principle: Every defender must be in advance of the ball. This beaten defender could only have occupied four positions: ball defender, first defender on weakside, second defender on weakside, or first strongside defender. We teach our players how to recover from each of these four areas.

Our basic rule, weakside defender must stop the loose dribbler, tells each defensive player where the dribbler will meet his next obstacle. Defenders respond accordingly.

If the ball defender has been faked and the dribbler drives by him, this defender continues beside the dribbler until he can either race back and recover (zig-zag drill) or until the weakside teammate approaches the dribbler. This weakside teammate tells the dribbler what he is to do. "Jump" tells the ball defender to rotate in the direction the weakside defender just left and find the open man (see Chapters 2 and 7). "Trap" would tell him to stay and double-team. If the ball handler picks up his dribble, "used" would dictate that the original ball defender must go in the direction that the weakside defender came from, looking for the open man. A number, such as 33, would activate the area man-to-man press (see Chapter 8); and the original ball defender would again rotate toward the deep weakside. The dribbler's original defender, in other words, either traps or rotates toward the weakside.

The first weakside defender may be too near a horizontal line with the dribbler to stop him (pursuant to the basic principle). In that case, he leaves his man and races downfloor on the dribbling-hand side of the dribbler, flicking away the ball if possible. Whenever his man moves, he must relocate him and defense him after the dribbler stops. However, if this defender can stop the dribbler immediately, either by hedging, jumping, switching, or flicking, it is his responsibility. If he stops the dribbler, the ball handler is his man. The original ball handler's defender takes this weakside man, unless a deeper weakside man shot the gap. Then the ball handler's original defender would take the deeper weakside attacker.

Should the ball handler manage to dribble past the first weakside defender, the second weakside defender must stop the ball. If he does not stop the dribbler, it would, in all probability, result in a lay-up. When the second weakside defender stops the ball, the dribbler becomes his man. This defender would force a lob or a bounce pass if the dribbler throws a quick pass to the man he just left (the obvious pass receiver). This pass might be deflected. Both, the ball handler's original man and the first weakside defender, should converge on the new pass receiver to stop a further move by him. The first one there takes this new pass receiver while the late defender takes the first weakside man (Diagram 1-6).

If the switching defender is the first strongside defender, he

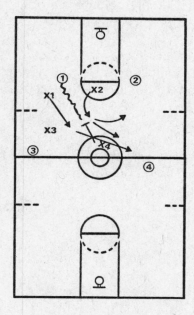

Diagram 1-6

would have stopped the ball. The ball handler's defender would then rotate toward the strongside defender (in the direction the ball is being dribbled). If the deeper weakside defender came over to pick up the first strongside attacker, the ball handler's defender would race to the weakside to find the man he would cover (Diagram 1-7).

The fifth man, the defensive safety, would stop the ball only as a last resort. He would then take the ball handler while the original ball defender would rotate to his man.

A full court defensive shell game drill is used to teach the defenders proper recovering angles and techniques when they are passed up by a dribbler. Complying with the above instruc- tions, X1, in all three diagrams (1-6 through 1-8), would follow the dribbler until he was stopped. When X1 hears "jump," he rotates in the direction of the dribble until he finds the open man.

In Diagram 1-6, X2 covers the dribble hand of 1, trying to flick the ball. X2 then covers either 2 or 4. X1 finds the man he is to cover by going down the line of the dribble, discovering who X2 has taken. X2's decision should rest on where he thinks 1 will pass the ball. X3 denies the pass to 3 because 3 is the first pass receiver on the ball side.

In Diagram 1-7, 1 drives to the outside. X3 must stop the dribbler. When X3 yells "jump," X1 goes toward 3 in the passing lane between 1 and 3, hoping to deflect any pass directed there. Should X1 find X4 on 3, then X1 goes toward 4. If X2 has chosen to cover 4, then X1 covers 2.

Diagram 1-8 illustrates a one-guard front. 1 drives by X1, and X2 comes too late to help. X2 tries to deflect the dribble away while moving in the direction of the dribbler. X4 comes hard to stop the dribbler. X2 chooses to cover 4 or 2. X1 covers 2 or 4, based on whom X2 covered. X3 could cover 4, forcing X1 to rotate to 3.

Procedure (Diagrams 1-6, 1-7, and 1-8):

1. Line players up as shown. After 1 has driven a few times, let 2 drive a few times as well. Rotate the front line defense to the back line and the back line to the front line. Then, switch offense to defense and repeat the process.

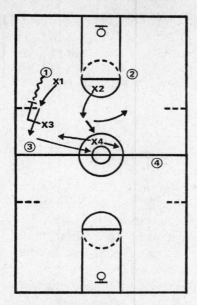

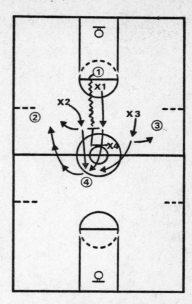

Diagram 1-7   **Diagram 1-8**

2. Coach should correct any violation of the fundamental principles (Chapter 5) as they occur.
3. If the drill is being used to teach the run and jump press (Chapter 7) or the area man-to-man press (Chapter 8), then any violation of the rules must be corrected immediately.
4. Begin drill by not permitting the attackers, other than the dribbler, to move. Then, let the others move in a straight line toward their offensive basket. After adequate progress, the attackers can move anywhere.
5. When the attackers successfully break the press, let them drive for the lay-up, teaching the defense to recover and prevent it.
6. When the defenders steal the pass, let them fast-break, teaching the quick conversion from offense to defense and from defense to offense.
7. Can use the drill for "trap" and "used" as well as "jump."

Objectives:
1. To teach proper rotation when passed up by a dribble.
2. To teach penetration and passing off against a press.

3. To teach defenders to read, to communicate, and to react to penetration by the dribble.
4. To teach many aspects of the run and jump press and area man-to-man press.
5. To teach quick conversions from offense to defense and from defense to offense.

SPACING

Proper spacing, an essential of successful pressing team defenses, must be individually maintained during each drill. Any defender guarding an attacker more than 20 feet from the ball or two men away from the ball should space himself two-thirds of the distance from the ball and one-third of the distance from his man. When guarding an attacker horizontally across from the ball, the defender should sink toward the dribbler, being able to stop a penetrating drive, but have a hand in the passing lane to the horizontal receiver. This would eliminate the direct chest pass. And when playing the next vertical pass receiver, the defender should play closer to the receiver in a denial stance, but still several feet away. If this vertical pass receiver steps toward this defender, the defender should step one-third of that distance away from the vertical receiver.

Anticipation and spacing are taught together in a three-on-four three-step drill. First, we teach the double-team or methods of trapping (see Chapter 2). Second, we combine this with shooting the gap (Chapter 2). Finally, we add the two deep men, 4 and X4 in Diagram 1-9, and begin emphasizing spacing. The first two drills will receive extensive coverage in Chapter 2. The third drill, on spacing, will be discussed here.

Procedure (Diagram 1-9);

1. Line players up as shown. Rotate from 1 to X1 to X2 to X3 to 3 to X4 to 4 to the end of the line.
2. After X1 and X2 have stopped 1's dribble, X2 can yell "jump," "trap," or "used," communicating to X1 his next responsibility. If "jump" or "used," X1 "fish hooks" back toward his defensive basket (see Chapter 2). If "trap," he double-teams with X2.
3. 1 can pass to either 3 or 4. 3 cannot come across the

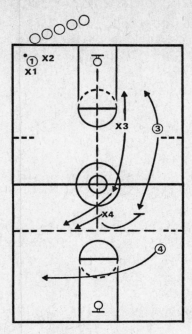

Diagram 1-9

half-court dotted line and 4 cannot come above the offensive 28-foot marker. X3 and X4 keep proper spacing
and try to shoot the gap to intercept any pass made to
their men.

4. Should 3 backdoor X3 and 1 throw 3 a long lob pass, X4
   must decide to either cover 4 or to try to draw the charge
   on 3. If X4 goes to draw the charge, X3 must rotate to 4.
   A completed pass brings a two-on-one game between 3
   and 4 and X3 and X4.
5. Any intercepted pass should result in a four-on-three
   fast break (X's against O's).

Objectives:
   1. To teach proper spacing.
   2. To teach anticipation.
   3. To help teach double-teaming and shooting the gap.
   4. To help teach X4 to draw the charge or force a violation
      on a backward-looking downfloor receiver.
   5. To help teach X3 to switch into the passing lane between

3 and 4 should X4 switch onto 3. X3's proper positioning would be directly between the passer and receiver, racing hard toward the intended receiver.

6. To teach conversion from defense to offense and from offense to defense.

PLAYING THE FIRST PASS RECEIVER

The receiver nearest the ball is the first pass receiver in that passing lane. He can locate in a passing lane inside 20 feet, outside 20 feet, or horizontal to the ball.

A defender whose man locates horizontally to the ball should sag and float. His position should enable him to keep a hand in the passing lane; yet he should prevent the ball handler from penetrating with a dribble in his direction. He should approximate one-third the distance from his man to the ball, and he should be about three feet from a line drawn through his man and the ball handler. This positioning should permit him to deflect the direct chest pass, to stop a dribbling penetration, and to force the slow bounce pass or the lob pass to his man cutting backdoor. But as his man cuts backdoor, he is becoming a vertical pass receiver.

Vertical pass receivers are divided into two categories: those inside 20 feet and those outside 20 feet. Different duties unfold for the different area positions.

Inside 20 feet, the defender denies all passes to the first pass receiver. He accomplishes this with a denial stance of a foot, arm, and head between his receiver and the ball. He has his back to the inside of the court. He locates two-thirds the distance from the ball. And should his man step toward him, he would retreat one-third the distance that his man advanced. This gives the defender a buffer zone from which he can successfully react to any quick move by his man or by the dribbler. It will also keep the defender close enough to his own man to deflect a lob pass.

Defenders on the first pass receiver inside 20 feet must also switch to a dribbler who has broken free. This creates a new and obvious passing lane to the first pass receiver. So as this defender switches to the dribbler, he should try to hinder or deflect this obvious pass.

Defenders outside 20 feet should sink to a spot toward mid-court where they could stop a cut to the ball by their own man, where they could deflect any direct chest pass, and where they could intercept any lob or bounce pass. This defender has much more time to see the penetrating dribbler advancing. Stopping the dribbler should pose no problem. But as he stops the dribbler, he should discourage the obvious pass to the man he just left. All the time, these defenders should physically float but mentally play the passing lane.

Should the defender's man cut away from the ball, the defender should prepare to switch men if a deeper defender yells "jump" (see next section). If the first pass receiver goes to screen for the second pass receiver, so the second pass receiver can break back to the ball, the first pass receiver's defender must communicate to his teammate: "slide," "switch," and so on.

PLAYING THE SECOND PASS RECEIVER

A second pass receiver is the second offensive attacker in any passing lane. Because another offensive receiver exists between the second pass receiver and the ball, denial defense need not be played. However, if this man moves within 20 feet of the passer, although another attacker is between him and the ball, the defender moves near the second pass receiver (two-thirds distance from the ball). If the second pass receiver locates outside 20 feet, his defender exaggerates his sag toward the center of the court, still being able to see both his man and the ball, being ever alert to stay close to his man if the second pass receiver intends to use a screen or tries to break toward the ball.

The defender on the second pass receiver has added responsibilities. Should the dribbler break past the front line of defense, this defender must stop him. If a lob pass is thrown to the first pass receiver, this defender can steal it, draw the charge near the point of reception, or force a walking violation with tight coverage at the point of reception. Should the second pass receiver race downfloor for a lob pass, his defender should be alert to a deeper defender calling "jump," which would require a switch.

From his initial exaggerated sag position in the middle of the floor, this defender can generally pick up any deflected ball or steal any poorly thrown pass. He may also consider "shooting the gap" on a pass to the first pass receiver when the first pass receiver's defender jumped the penetrating dribbler.

If the first pass receiver comes to screen the second pass receiver's defender so that his man can break back toward the ball, this defender must react to the call of the first pass receiver's defender. But if the second pass receiver's defender is alert, he should easily avoid the screen.

PLAYING THE THIRD PASS RECEIVER

Attacking formations rarely place three offensive players in the same passing lane. But it sometimes happens in the course of a game.

Defenders on the third pass receiver have a golden opportunity to float to the middle of the floor and draw charges on all cutting players. This defender's main area of emphasis should be the passing lane and helping his teammates. He has opportunities to shoot the gap or rotate to an obvious pass receiver in the run and jump maneuvers. He should challenge all lob pass receivers.

Dribblers should concern this defender only in rare cases. He must stop a free dribbler, but none should reach him. A dribbler must defeat three other defenders to approach him.

But when the third pass receiver moves within 20 feet of the ball, his defender must eliminate his exaggerated sag and close to within two-thirds the distance of the ball. He must do this even when his man remains the third attacker in a passing lane. Closing to that distance not only prevents his man from receiving a direct pass, but it allows the defender to initiate our man-to-man press stunts (see Chapters 6, 7, and 8).

PLAYING THE FOURTH PASS RECEIVER

Teams that align four players in a single passing lane grant exaggerated sag and extraordinary recovery powers to the defender on that fourth pass receiver. That defender would float even further away from his man and toward the center court than the third pass receiver's defender. His responsibilities would be the same, except the fourth pass receiver's defender would be the safety, the last line of defense.

As safety he must not stop a loose dribbler high and away from the basket unless he sees a teammate nearby who can defend the area of the basket. If the offense outnumbers the safety and it appears they will obtain the lay-up, the safety should commit the smart foul, preventing not only the easy two but the three-point play. An example of a smart foul: A breakaway dribbler is driving toward his basket. The safety can leave his man and try to gain position on the driver, hoping to draw the charge. If he succeeds, he gains a possession for his team. If he establishes his position too late and a block is called, he saves the easy lay-up which would follow a pass to the man the safety just left. But if the driver is attempting the lay-up, the safety should try for a steal. If contact is made, the safety must be sure to foul both arms, preventing the three-point play.

If it is the fifth foul and the defender is indispensable, we would not advocate this foul. In all situations, rather than fouling, we prefer delaying the shot until defensive help arrives. Neither should the safety foul the jump shooter, but he must deny any 100 percent two-pointers (the lay-up).

If the safety is a good shot blocker, a la Bill Russell style, you should teach him to block with the near hand. As the driver goes by the safety, the safety turns to face the basket. His hand nearest the driver when in this facing-the-basket stance must be used to block the shot. This enables the safety to protect the inside for a return pass and the ensuing lay-up; and it enables him to block the ball off of the board if shot, thereby keeping it in play.

RECOVERING WHEN PASSED UP BY A PASS

A cardinal principle of our defense (Chapter 5) requires every defender to react as the ball is thrown, not after it has been received. Three seconds will elapse on all semi-lob full court passes, and it takes about three seconds for a defender to run the length of the court. A defender who locates 20 or 30 feet ahead of the passer certainly would have no trouble recovering. All defenders should arrive ahead of any diagonally thrown semi-lob pass. Defenders, therefore, have enough time to recover on any semi-lob pass. And the pass must at least be semi-lobbed if the defender on the ball has played the dribbler properly (see earlier part of this chapter).

Certain small details allow us even greater recovery. The defender on the passer must pivot in the direction of the pass, using the opposite foot as his pivot foot, and take a long step, pushing off his pivot foot, and racing hard to get ahead of the ball. His route should take him down the center of the court. He should run a straight line toward the basket he is defending. He should not watch the flight of the ball.

The pass receiver's defender must race toward the point of reception. He should have his body between the receiver and the center court lane. This technique permits him to cover the receiver; or if he hears "jump," he can rotate more quickly to the next open man.

The other three defenders, those not involved with the passer or the receiver, should race down the midcourt lane, but on the same side as the receiver. This prevents another cutter from breaking between the new pass receiver and the cutter's defender. Only another lob pass could be successful. And should the new pass receiver decide to dribble-drive, the well-positioned defenders can help prevent the dribbling penetration. From this positioning defenders can fan out away from the basket to pick up their man.

Of course, if a defender is ahead of the point of reception, he may leave his man, race to the point of reception, yell "jump," try to draw the charge, or force the violation. This defender would now defend the new pass receiver. And his job, momentarily, would be control of the new receiver. The new pass receiver must not be permitted to abruptly advance the ball. Even a moment's delay would grant more than enough recovery time for an alert defender.

The anticipation and spacing drill is used to teach the important recovery concepts. Another attacker and defender on the ball side, Diagram 1-10, is added. This defender and the two double-teamers must race to get above any pass directed downcourt.

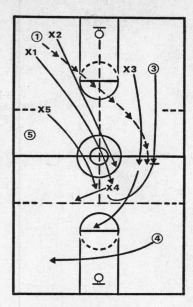

Diagram 1-10

Procedure (Diagram 1-10):

1. Line up four offensive and five defensive players as shown.
2. When 1 passes to either 3, 4, or 5, X1, X2, and either X3 or X5 must race to get above the ball before the new pass receiver can catch it.
3. X2 would operate as the passer's defender, and X1 would become run man seeking to find his new man. He would use the container's rotation techniques.
4. In Diagram 1-10, X3 would be the pass receiver's defender. X4 would be the defender above the point of reception. Both would use their recovery coverage techniques.
5. When the new pass receiver receives the ball, he should immediately try to advance it. His defender should try to prevent this.

Objectives:

1. To teach defenders the proper angles to recovering when passed up by a pass.

2. To teach anticipation and spacing.
3. To teach passing and receiving under pressure.
4. To teach double-teaming and shooting the gaps.
5. To teach drawing the charge, forcing the violation, jumping, and so on.
6. To teach repicking up correct assignments if the pass is completed.

HOW TO PICK UP THE LOOSE MAN

Only three types of loose attackers offer immediate threats: the cutter, the new pass receiver, and the dribbler. Methods of coverage for each differ somewhat.

Cutters can cause the ultimate damage against a press. That damage comes when they receive a pass; consequently, we deny them the ball. All our drills are designed to force the cutter behind his defender. This requires the passer to see through at least two defenders to find the cutter. And even after finding him, only a semi-lob pass would be successful. The semi-lob pass, unless perfectly thrown, invites an interception. If the defender chooses not to intercept, he can activate another harassing stunt as the new pass receiver receives the ball. And any defender on the same side of the court as the backdoor cutter can draw the charge, especially if the cutter looks backward as he cuts, or force a walking violation when this cutter receives the pass.

Defenders of new pass receivers must reach the point of reception before the ball arrives. If the defender can deflect the pass, he should slap the ball toward the center of the court where all the defenders are retreating. If he cannot deflect the lob, he should be within inches of the new receiver. His inside foot should be near the defensive basket. His hands should be out, ready to tie up the receiver. Most receivers who run to catch lob passes bring the ball down to their waist before making another move. Other receivers immediately receive the ball and begin dribbling. The defender has perfect positioning to draw the charge. Unpoised receivers, when they see the tight defender, will walk, trying to avoid the contact, especially if they have extended themselves and therefore are not under perfect body control.

Defenders must approach dribblers with caution. They should run at the dribbler under control, playing slightly (half-man) to one side. That side should correspond to the side of the court where the defender just came from. This serves a dual purpose: It places the defender in the next obvious passing lane, and such coverage would permit that defender to deflect a pass thrown there; and it forces the dribbler in only one direction, the opposite direction from which he is currently dribbling. This activates the zig-zag drill for the defender who must now bring the dribbler under control. Also, the dribbler may have to change his direction into his original defender. A behind-the-back or reverse dribble should be stolen by the original defender while the crossover should be stolen by the new defender. The dribbler will probably pick up the ball and look for someone new to pass to. The defense will be rotating into the new passing lanes.

WATCH FLOOR POSITION

Good man-to-man defenders always know where the ball is and where their men are. Great defenders also know their position on the court.

Floor position includes a thorough knowledge of the best areas to trap (see Chapter 2), of the passing lanes from each region of the floor (see Chapter 2), and of the better gambling areas. Diagram 1-11 depicts the latter. The dotted line should not represent a rigid boundary, but a general one. Players must decide how elastic the dotted line can be by contrasting their own speed and that of the men they guard. Generally speaking, however, the chart lists the gambling duties of defenders in the four areas.

Area 1:

1. Defenders on the ball must cover their man so tightly that the attacker cannot pass safely and will begin to dribble.

2. Defenders off of the ball can gamble wildly on interceptions.
3. Defenders off of the ball can initiate run and jumps.
4. All defenders must race to get ahead of the ball if passed up by a dribble or a pass.

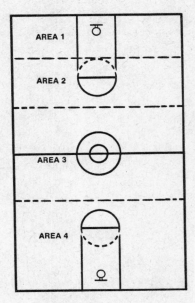

Diagram 1-11

Area 2:

1. Defenders off of the ball can gamble excessively.
2. Defenders on the ball must play their man tightly, forcing a dribble.
3. Defenders off of the ball can draw a charge off of the cutters from Area 1.
4. Defenders off of the ball can initiate run and jumps, as well as shoot the gaps in Areas 1 and 2.
5. Defenders off of the ball must keep passes out of the middle lane.
6. All defenders must be alert to get back ahead of the ball if they are passed up by a dribble or pass.

Area 3:

1. Defenders off of the ball can draw charges on all cutters from Areas 1 and 2.
2. Defenders off of the ball can switch men on run and jumps, either as an initiator or as a gap shooter.
3. Defenders off of the ball can bother lob pass receivers, either deflecting, intercepting, or drawing a charge.
4. Defenders off of the ball must be observant to pick up a loose dribbler or a loose cutter.
5. Defenders off of the ball can gamble on intercepting passes. They can gamble more if teammates are in Areas 3 or 4.
6. All defenders must never allow a pass into the middle lane.

Area 4:

1. No defender must ever leave his man unless he is reasonably sure that a teammate can cover the basket area for him.
2. Defender off of the ball can float to middle and deflect passes that he has a 50-50 chance of getting.
3. Defender can leave his man to shoot gap or draw charge on a lob pass receiver, if a teammate can cover his man or can recover to defend the basket area.

HOW TO TEACH PLAYERS TO ANALYZE AND REACT

The more imaginative picture puzzles defenders' minds can conjure up and the better and more often these defenders can solve these puzzles, the quicker they begin to analyze and react. A coach cannot make the defenders' instant decisions for them. He must rely on their judgment, and the outcome of a game often hinges on the sum total of those decisions.

So, coaches must teach their defenders to analyze and react better and quicker. There are a multitude of methods for instilling this savvy. Drills used by the coach, especially the ones presented in this book, is one way. Players can watch videotapes of their practices, seeing when they should react and how.

Films of college games offer another opportunity. "Chalk" talks help. Television presents several games each week. On off-nights players can watch other local high schools perform.

But watching games alone will not suffice. A player must have an assigned responsibility if he is to gain maximum benefit. We ask our players to study the offensive team's methods of attacks. We ask them to record where they could have run and jumped, where they could have drawn a charge on a cutter or forced a violation from a lob pass receiver, and so on. As a defensive player begins to study and analyze different games, he begins to get a better mental picture of what the opposition can do and when they will do it.

A DENIAL PRESSURE AND PASSING LANE DRILL

When the first pass receiver in any passing lane locates within 20 feet of the passer, his defender denies him the ball. When a receiver resides outside of 20 feet, his defender would sag, forcing a lob pass, offering help to those covering the passing lanes.

Procedure (Diagram 1-12):
1. 1 has the ball. He does not have a dribble.
2. X1 pressures 1.
3. 1 may pass to 2 or 3. X2 and X3 prevent the direct chest or bounce pass to 2 or 3 by keeping a hand in the passing lane.
4. 2 and 3 can move within ten feet of the passer and as far away as they like. But if 2 or 3 move farther than 20 feet away, 4 or 5 must break toward 1, except when 2 or 3 race after a lob pass.
5. 4 and 5 locate outside of 20 feet. X4 and X5 sag. X4 and X5 must cover a lob pass directed to 2, 3, 4, or 5.
6. 2 and 3 could screen for 4 or 5. Coach can have 2, 3, 4, and 5 operate as their next opponent would.

Objectives:
1. To teach proper denial coverage.
2. To teach proper passing lane coverage.

3. To teach coverage of the lob passes.
4. After teaching proper rotation drills, X2 and X3 must rotate with X4 and X5 on coverage of lob passes.
5. To teach the little mechanics described throughout this chapter.

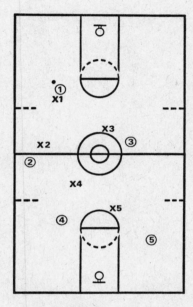

Diagram 1-12

2

Coaching
Different Methods of
Trapping and Switching

After each individual defender becomes proficient at defending his man and knowledgeable about his role and duties in rotating to that man, instruction should turn toward developing team principles. The first step in teaching team tenets involves tutoring the cooperative techniques between two defenders. Knowledge of traps, switching, and their allied mechanics, therefore, becomes a principal part of pressing and the subject of this chapter.

HEDGING

Coaches can classify hedging as a defensive fake instead of a defensive stunt. But when the defense couples hedging with the run and jump or another switching stunt, it can have the same effect on the dribbler and his receivers as the stunts.

Hedging, the art of faking a run and jump toward a dribbler but recovering on one's own man, is run only by the first pass receiver's defender. This defender calls the hedging move at his own discretion. Other defenders notice and react to the hedger's call.

To hedge, the defensive player should drop his denial foot out of the denial passing lane toward the middle lane (Diagram 2-1), squaring his shoulder toward the guard who is driving at

55

him. The defender should then jab a step or two toward the
dribbler, but all the time being able to retreat back to his own
man.

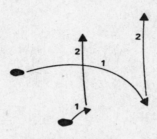

Diagram 2-1

This original drop step by the denial foot and the sub-
sequent jab steps key the hedger's teammates that he is hedging
and not running and jumping or starting some stunt. This gives
the defender's teammates the impression that he is hesitating.
And, in our stunts, we want an instant decision without any
hesitation. We want the defender who activates a stunt to race
toward the dribbler, not jab step toward him.

After a few run and jumps or other team defensive feats, the
attackers cannot be sure. It creates an illusion that another trap
or stunt might be forthcoming. The dribbler might pick up the
ball, and this would initiate our dribble "used" drill. Or the
dribbler might hurriedly throw a backdoor lob pass to the
hedger's man, thinking the hedger was coming to trap him. The
hedger should be able to deflect or steal such a pass.

Any defender who has a dribbler driving toward him may
call the hedge. His teammates must read the hedge and act
accordingly.

Hedgers hedge to slow down a dribbler so the dribbler's
defender can better control him. It can force the dribbling attacker to veer his route a little farther outside, permitting a
beaten defender to recover. It can cause an unpoised and frequently trapped dribbler to pick up his dribble or to throw a
hasty backdoor pass. It can keep the dribbler off-balance, especially when hedging has been coupled with traps and stunts.

However, it also impels the hedger's man to make a decision. If this potential pass receiver suspects a trap, he will break

back toward the ball, making it easier for this defender to run and jump two widely separated attackers. If this first pass receiver reads the defensive performance as the hedging move, he will become a cutter, keeping his eye on the dribbler for a lob backdoor pass. Teammates of the hedger should draw a charge off such a cutter. When a deeper defender sees a teammate hedging, this cues that deep defender to get into position to steal the backdoor lob pass, to draw the charge on the non-looking backdoor cutter, or to force a walking violation at the point of reception. Any such maneuver by the deeper defender calls for the hedger to switch to the deeper defender's man. The deeper defender, naturally, would cover the hedger's man.

FLOATING

Defensive players whose men locate farther than 20 feet from the ball float. The farther the attackers move away from the ball the farther their defenders can float. This conforms to the axiom: Float on players more than one pass away (Chapter 5).

These are physical floats. We want our floaters to mentally play the passing lanes (another basic precept in Chapter 5). Of course, the floater must mentally play the lane to his man. His position is one step off a line between his man and the ball per 20 feet. And he is two-thirds the distance from the ball to his man, with his back to the middle lane.

This positioning gives him the ideal location to mentally play all the other possible passing lanes, as well as the passing lane to his own man. Floaters' duties are not restricted to coverage of their own men, but they must help on all defensive maneuvers that occur in front of them. They should help on any lob pass thrown to a cutter when the point of reception is in front of them. They should help the hedger when the hedger's man cuts backdoor. They must stop any dribbler who has managed to get by the front line of defense. They must make an instant decision whether to rotate to an open pass receiver or stay with their own man when the teammates in front of them initiate a run and jump. However, if the floater is the deepest defender, he must play safety, a position which demands less gambling.

Hedgers and floaters usually pick up their duties quickly. But for those who do not, we have a hedgers and floaters drill.

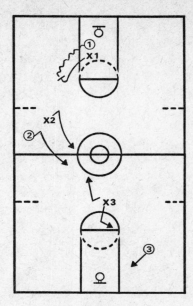

Diagram 2-2

Procedure (Diagram 2-2):

1. Line up three offensive and three defensive players. Rotate in a clockwise manner.
2. 1 begins drill by dribbling toward X2. X1 tries hurriedly to catch up and reestablish position on 1.
3. X2 either hedges or runs and jumps. If working on hedging, 1 must slow down and throw a lob pass to either 2 or 3.
4. If X3 comes up to cover a pass thrown to 2, X2 would, when he hears "jump," race to cover 3.
5. When working on a run and jump X2 would race directly toward 1, forcing 1 to halt his dribble or pass the ball. X3 must decide to cover either 2 or 3. X1 can trap with X2 on 1, or X1 can race back toward 2 to cover 2 or circle on around to cover 3 (Diagram 2-17).
6. When passed up by a pass, all defenders, such as X1, must race down the middle court lane to get ahead of the ball. Any deflected lob pass should be directed toward that center lane.

Objectives:

1. To teach hedging and floating.
2. To teach proper rotations when running a defensive stunt.
3. To teach backdoor cut and lob pass options to the offense.
4. To teach retreating when passed up by a pass.
5. To teach deflecting passes back into center court lane (where defensive teammates are .

DOUBLE-TEAMING

Double-teaming occurs at different spots and different intervals in the man-to-man press. Unlike its zone counterpart, man-to-man double-teaming is a spontaneous reply to an offensive question.

Because of this lack of pre-planned spots, all man-to-man defenders must be adept at double-teaming as well as reading when their teammates intend to double-team. Basically, man-to-man defenders can double-team the crossing of the ball and two offensive players, and anytime a dribbler is dribbling toward another defender who is 20 feet or less away.

As this defender (20 feet or less away) approaches the dribbler, he should study the situation. If he feels he can force the dribbler to pick up the dribble or throw a bad pass, he should yell "used" (picked-up dribble) or "jump" (thrown bad pass). This keys the defender who originally guarded the dribbler to rotate to the next open man. The defender who was 20 feet or less away stays with the original dribbler. That is our double-teaming rule. We call the original dribbler's defender the container, and the defender 20 feet or less away, in our vernacular, is the trapper. The trapper always stays with the man he goes after and the container always rotates.

If the trapper wants help from the container in the double-team, he yells "trap." We want the trap set against any unpoised passer, against the player who the offensive coach has designated as his ball handler, against the attacking team late in a game we are losing, against all teams at different intervals for variety, and against the attacking team when we have scored after just stealing the ball.

There are two ways that double-teamers can steal the ball: steal the pass when thrown out of the trap, or tie up or steal the ball while it is still in the trap. The former is the best since the latter leads to fouling, a foul that permits the offense to escape from a difficult situation. To force the bad pass, defenders should first permit the attacker to dribble then apply the double-team. This eliminates one of the offensive moves. After he has started dribbling, we want the trapper to approach him with caution, never allowing him to split us with a dribble. Once the offensive man has lost his dribble, we assume a tight, narrow base. The narrow base is important; it encourages the bounce pass. Our inside feet are perpendicular to each other. Our outside arms are high, and our inside arms are located at the knee and the shoulder. Our arms are waved in a constant windmilling motion.

Because of the positioning of our feet and our inside arms, it is almost impossible for the offensive man to step through the area between us. He will make a bounce pass around us or throw a lob pass over us.

The offensive man could leave his feet. If he does we leave ours. The attacker cannot come down with the ball without walking. We try to deflect a level pass, forcing the lob.

If we try to steal the ball while it is in the trap (we do not encourage this), we want to slap up at the ball. We want the defender to move his body toward the ball, keeping his hand on it by sheer hustle. This will give us a jump ball and we will try to recover the ensuing tip.

If the defender can get both hands on the ball, he should immediately begin a steady pull and then suddenly jerk down. The moment the defensive man feels his opponent giving, the defender should use his body as a lever to pry the ball loose.

We use several drills to teach double-teaming, and each will be presented in the areas where we discuss that method of team defense. This drill helps perfect our approach and our stance. We call it our double-teaming drill.

Procedure (Diagram 2-3):

1. Line players up in one line. Rotate from 1 to X1 to X2 to the end of the line.

2. Coach passes to 1 to activate the drill.
3. 1 tries to break the double-team by dribbling.
4. X1 tries to contain 1 until X2 arrives for the double-team.
5. 1 keeps dribble alive while X1 and X2 force him into the corner. We like 1 to keep dribbling because it causes X1 and X2 to force him into the corner. This eliminates reaching in and fouling while trying to steal the dribble when double-teaming, a cardinal defensive sin.

Objectives:

1. To teach dribbler to avoid the double-team.
2. To teach how to double-team correctly.
3. To teach one defender how to contain and another how to apply the trap. X1 prevents vertical advancement; X2 eliminates horizontal movement.

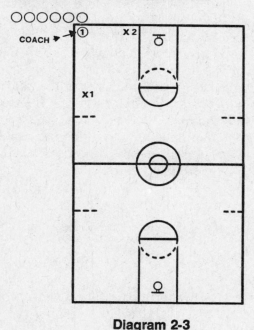

Diagram 2-3

THE LOOSE TRAP AND THE TIGHT TRAP

Two defenders can apply a loose trap or a tight, narrow-based trap. When the dribbler likes to throw a quick pass as he sees the trap approaching, or when the dribbler likes to keep his dribble alive by attempting to loop out of the trap, the defenders should use a loose trap. But should the attacker be prone to picking up his dribble as he sees the approaching trap, the defenders would use the tight trap. If the attacker has his dribble left, we would use the loose trap. This last situation rarely occurs in a man-to-man press because the trapper does not go after the man with the ball until he dribbles toward the trapper.

Defenders, one to stop horizontal advancement and one to contain vertically, stay three to five feet from the dribbler in the loose trap. This not only enables the defenders to deflect babied passes, but it makes the passer have to lob the ball higher or bounce the pass shorter in order to get it by the loose trap. That aids the gap shooters in stealing the pass. These two defenders must make themselves appear big by keeping their legs spread and their arms up and waving. This keeps the dribbler from seeing his pass receiver well. This spread trap also keeps the looping dribbler from escaping.

Tight traps, used on attackers who pick up their dribble, force the bounce or lob pass. Defenders know that the dribbler cannot pick up his pivot foot and return it to the floor without walking. The narrow base gives the passer the bounce pass, a very slow pass. The windmill waving grants the lob pass, another slow pass. The tight trap helps unnerve the passer and keeps pressure on him even if the trapper releases the container by the word "used."

RESPONSIBILITY OF THE CONTAINER

Container, in our vocabulary, means the defender on the dribbler. The container must contain or keep the dribbler under control. He must never permit the dribbler to advance the ball vertically without harassment. He must channel the dribbler toward the trap, which may be spontaneously called by the trapper ("help" lets the container know where the trapper is) or pre-arranged by the coach. He must tightly or loosely trap when the trapper yells "trap." He must rotate until he finds the open receiver by going down the line of the dribble when he hears "used" or "jump" from the trapper. After the trapper yells "jump" or "trap," the container must prevent the dribbler from advancing the ball horizontally.

RESPONSIBILITY OF THE TRAPPER

Trappers leave their designated man to come to the ball and help the container control the dribbler. Any defender within 20 feet of the ball becomes a potential trapper. When the dribbler dribbles toward a defender within 20 feet, he invites the trap. Trappers should run directly at the dribbler with arms up and waving, but body under control. They must remain cautious of a splitting dribble move. Trappers must never let the dribbler advance the ball in the direction from which they came. A trapper must size up the situation where the ball, container, and he himself converge, calling either "jump," "used," or "trap." He should vary his calls in relation to what the team has been doing, thereby keeping the attackers guessing.

Trappers call "jump" when they suspect the obvious pass (a pass to the man they just left), when they expect the dribbler to pick up his dribble, or when facing an unpoised dribbler. "Used" sends the container out of a trap into the passing lanes. "Used" means the dribbler has picked up his dribble. Trappers call "trap" when they want double-team help from the container. Trappers can trap until the dribbler picks up his dribble, then they can require the container to leave the trap by "used."

The trapper takes the original dribbler after he yells "trap," "used," or "jump." A pass followed by a middle cut could free the original dribbler. So the trapper must jump toward any pass thrown out of the double-team, thereby preventing the middle cut.

TRAP AFTER LOSS OF DRIBBLE

After a dribbler picks up the dribble, both the loose and the tight trap can be employed. The tight trap has the advantage of unnerving the attacker, forcing a quicker pass. The loose trap, however, prevents the man who had been trapped from breaking by the trapper for a quick return pass. Alternating the loose trap with the tight trap can be almost as effective as switching defenses.

TRAP BEFORE LOSS OF DRIBBLE

Defenders must play the attacker with the ball loosely until he loses his dribble. Unless it is called from the bench, defenders do not trap a pass receiver until that receiver begins his dribble. But when we do trap the pivoting, stationary player with the ball who has not dribbled, we trap loosely, trying to appear big to limit his downcourt vision and trying to force a soft pass (lob or bounce) that the double-teamer's teammates can intercept. We do not permit this attacker to step between us and begin a dribble.

If a player is already dribbling, the container (the dribbler's defender) and the trapper try to force him to pick up his dribble. These two defenders keep the dribbler from advancing horizontally or vertically while trying to force him to retreat. In Diagram 2-3, for example, X1 and X2 would force 1 to exit through the corner or pick up his dribble. After the dribbler picks up his dribble, the trapper has three options: He may defense the ex-dribbler alone and send the container into the passing lanes with "used"; he may tightly double-team with the container by initiating tight coverage; or he may loosely double-team with the container by loosely playing the ex-dribbler.

BEST TIMES TO TRAP

Full court pressure man-to-man defensive teams do not always trap. They can jump or use assorted stunts which leave the ball handler covered by one individual defender.

Each game, however, offers moments when traps become mandatory. Defensive teams should exploit periods of offensive and defensive momentum by trapping. Any successful trap which results in a steal and a quick basket should be followed by another trap. This brings about a frenzied atmosphere to which unpoised ball handlers will succumb. A dribbler who insists upon turning his back to the downcourt area as he brings the ball up the floor should be easy prey to a double-team. If the trap is set just as the dribbler turns, the ball is easily stolen or the dribbler will walk.

Late in a quarter with only a few seconds left, an offensive attack can be slowed, even halted, by a successful trap. At the least, some defensive stunt should be tried to prevent the easy last-second shot.

When a good ball handler has been picking the defense apart, either by clever passing or expert dribbling and driving, the defense should force him to give up the ball before he does considerable damage. A trap offers a solution. When this ball handler does pass off, the trapper would face-guard him, never allowing him to get the ball back. The container, under our rules, would leave the trap to find the next open man.

BEST AREAS OF COURT FOR TRAPPING

Where passing lanes are fewer in number, the defense finds its best area to trap. Area 1, in Diagram 2-4, allows the passer only three passing lanes: to the left, to the right, and down the middle. Area 2 adds another: the backward passing lane. And Area 3 adds a sideline passing lane to Area 2. 1, 2, and 3, in that order, are the best areas in which to trap.

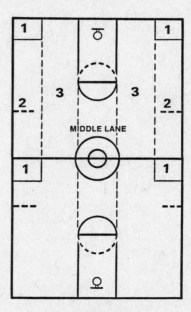

Diagram 2-4

Trapping in the center lane should be discouraged since a passer has eight lanes, and the defense only has three men to cover those lanes. Stunts which leave one defender on the dribbler work better for the defense in the center lane. Perhaps, the stunt might even force the dribbler toward Area 3.

HOW TO RECOGNIZE AND COVER PASSING LANES

Mentally draw a horizontal and a vertical lane through the attacker in a trap. That gives four passing lanes: backward and forward to the left and right. Split each of these quadrants with a 45° angle and it results in eight passing lanes (Diagram 2-5). Because of the lines on the court, Area 1 makes only three of those passing lanes available. Area 2 only adds the backward two lanes. Area 3 adds the other horizontal lanes and the two 45° lanes, but most teams do not send a cutter up the sideline (Area 2) where 3 is stopped. The center lane, however, exposes all eight lanes.

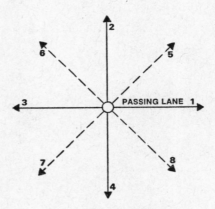

Diagram 2-5

Defensive players can quickly picture the lanes, but they often fail to cover them. Each defender plays his man physically, but he should mentally cover the nearest passing lane as well. If they do this, all lanes with any attacker nearby will be covered. If there are no attackers in that lane, then it would not be covered. However, there is no need to cover a lane where there is no receiver.

Defenders too often give up physical coverage on their man, concentrating on a passing lane. This gives the passer an outlet. Or they will concentrate on their man, failing to deflect a pass into a nearby lane.

Defenders must learn to use an open stance and make themselves appear big, unless their assigned man is within 20 feet of the passer and occupies one of the direct passing lanes. In that case, the defender uses a closed denial stance, preventing the direct pass. In the former case, the open stance, the defender would be zoning it, one-third of the distance from his man to the ball and one step off the line drawn from his man to the ball for every 20 feet his man is away from the ball.

JUMP TRAP

When two attackers and the ball converge at a single point, the defense can activate the jump trap. Diagram 2-6 depicts 1 using 2 as a screener, attempting to drive around 2. X2 has two possible routes. He located himself between 1 and 2 originally, preventing the direct vertical pass from 1 to 2. If X2 likes, he

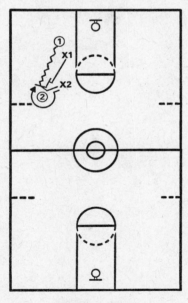

Diagram 2-6

may swing in front of 2 with a quick step out in front of the driving 1. Or, X2 could pretend coverage of 2, swinging behind 2 and at the last moment stepping out in front of the driving 1. Going in front of 2 leaves 2 open for the obvious pass a fraction of a second longer. But it stops the dribbler quicker and shows the defender's teammates his intentions earlier. Going behind 2 is a sudden and more surprise move to 1. Both have their advantages and disadvantages and we indeed use both.

When X2 jumps in front of 1, he must align his right shoulder even with 1's right shoulder; and he must have his nose on the ball. Sometimes more than one step is required to get this favorable positioning. X2 must yell "trap," informing X1 to stay for the double-team.

When X2 places his nose on the ball, 1 must change direction or charge. X1 should prevent the change of direction. If X2 suspects a quick obvious pass (pass to 2), he can remain semi-upright, rotating his arms in an attempt to deflect the ball. If he suspects a change of direction, his trail hand should be low to steal the crossover. A reverse would charge into X1. A behind-the-back is easily stolen by X1.

JUMPING OUT AND SHOWING

Jumping out and showing is really a hedging maneuver, but we include it here with the traps because it looks like the jump trap. When used shortly after the jump trap has been used, the dribbler will pick up his dribble. If the dribbler has been making the obvious pass (to 2 in Diagram 2-6), he will have it intercepted by X2.

To jump out and show, X2 does exactly as he did in the jump trap—but without calling "trap." His silence tells X1 that he is to stay with 1. X2 intends to recover on his own man. X2, after jumping out, pauses only for a moment before retreating into the passing lane between 1 and 2.

X2 can better jump and show if he goes behind 2. 2 has fewer seconds that he remains open, and X2 could get into the passing lane quicker.

HEDGING FOLLOWED BY A TRAP

Jump trapping, blitz trapping, and the long run and jump trapping techniques work well after a hedge. The regular run and jump trap works better without hedging, but it will work following a hedge as well. However, hedging-then-trapping may confuse a third run and jump defender who wants to get involved (see Chapter 7). As long as it remains a two-man stunt, even run and jump, the defense can thoroughly confuse the offense by hedging-then-trapping.

After hedging a few times and trapping a few times, the dribbler could begin to recognize the difference in the two. A hedge followed by a trap would perplex that thinking dribbler.

Hedging-then-trapping impels the dribbler to slow his dribble when he sees the next hedge, since he will not be sure if it is a trap or a hedge. He will not be sure for the remainder of the game. Hedging-then-trapping also eliminates the quick obvious pass, for the dribbler can never be sure when the hedger's man will be open.

To hedge-then-trap the defender must make a realistic trapping (such as run and jump) motion at a dribbler coming toward him. Then he must slowly, but effectively, take a few controlled steps back toward his own man. Then with catlike quickness and with authoritative speed he must explode directly toward the dribbler, making himself as big as possible, even yelling "trap," "trap," "trap."

This action should disconcert the dribbler momentarily, helping the ball handler's defender control the dribbler and helping his teammates fill the passing lanes. The obvious pass should be deflected; the continued dribble should be stolen (see Chapter 1).

BLITZ TRAP

Traps are more successful against a dribbler. Before an attacker begins his dribble, he has an extra option and that option can free him from a trap.

There are times, however, when it becomes necessary to trap the stationary attacker who has his dribble left. A quick trap on the in-bounds pass receiver—either late in the game when the defense is behind or after successfully scoring from the previous trap, which may create the frenzied effect—offers one good example. Teams that clear out the backcourt for one attacker before beginning the dribble is another good example.

A blitz trap is executed before the attacker dribbles. Because the attacker can fake before he dribbles, he must be approached with extreme care. The container, defender on the attacker with the ball, should be several feet away from his man. The trapper should get to the receiver as he receives the ball, if possible. If it is not possible, the trapper should race to a few feet of the potential dribbler and then approach him under control.

Diagram 2-7 displays the immediate blitz trap on the in-bounds pass receiver. We expect this trap if we just scored from a trapping situation. X1's first move is to recover to a horizontal even position to 2. Many times he can achieve this as 2 receives the ball. While X2 prevents 2 from faking and driving vertically, X1 must prevent the fake and drive horizontally.

Diagram 2-8 depicts the clearout by 1. When 1 gets 20 feet away from 2, X1 races back to within a few feet of 2 with his hands up, deflecting any careless pass back to the obvious receiver, 1. X1 must force either the lob or the bounce pass if 2 chooses to give up the ball. Going 20 feet back with 1 gives X1's teammates an opportunity to cover 1. Should 2 keep the ball and try to dribble by X1 and X2, the two defenders launch the double-teaming drill (Diagram 2-3).

X1, if he suspects a clearout, can immediately blitz trap (Diagram 2-7); or he can accept the clearout then blitz trap (Diagram 2-8). These two options offer more versality to the man-to-man press.

RUN AND JUMP TRAP

The run and jump trap is originated by any defender within 20 feet of the dribbler, provided the dribbler is dribbling toward the trapper. Fifteen feet or less provides for even better results.

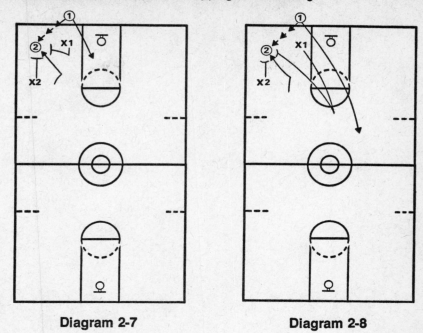

Diagram 2-7   Diagram 2-8

In the front court, a trapper must be within ten feet, preferably less. Trappers, X2 in Diagram 2-9, must align themselves directly in the line that the attacker is dribbling. In other words, the routes of X2 and 1 must make a straight line. 1's view of the obvious pass is hindered by X2's apparent bigness and his arm-waving. X2, however, must come hard and fast at the shoulder of 1's dribbling arm. If he switches dribbling hands, X1 would have no trouble stealing the ball. X2 would have a half-a-man over-play, preventing 1 from advancing directly. If X2 yells "jump," he would be calling the run and jump switch, covered in a later section in this chapter. If he yells "trap," X1 stays and traps with X2. Should 1 successfully pass out of the trap, X1 would switch to 2 unless another defender had come to cover 2; then X1 would rotate until he finds the open man (see section on Responsibility of the Container). Should 1 try to keep his dribble alive, X1 and X2 institute the double-teaming drill.

When X2 decides to run and jump trap or switch, his decision must show no hesitation. He must aggressively charge the dribbler, otherwise he would confuse his reacting teammates.

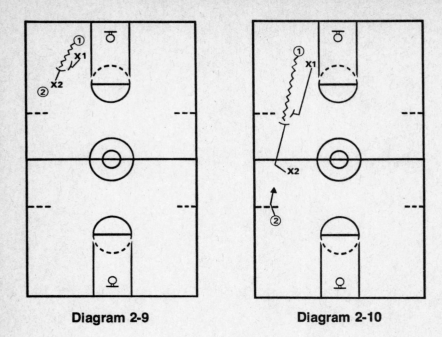

Diagram 2-9   **Diagram 2-10**

LONG RUN AND JUMP TRAP

Like the run and jump, the long run and jump requires the dribbler to move toward the jumper. The difference is in the distance the jumper runs to start the trap and in the method the container uses to channel the dribbler toward the trapper.

Traps from the long run and jumps occur exclusively in Area 2 (Diagram 2-4). Any other area would give the dribbler too large a region to operate in. It would therefore be most difficult for the trapper to control the dribbler, and the trapper's defensive teammates could not adjust to the open man.

X1, in Diagram 2-10, must back off 1 a few feet toward the middle lane. X1 must also stay about half a step in front of 1. When X1's teammates see this positioning, they know the long run and jump is called. X2 races hard toward 1. Because of X2's distance from 1, 1 cannot pass quickly to the obvious pass receiver, 2. 1 must lob the ball. It must be a high semi-lob to get the ball over X2. X1 must prevent the horizontal pass, and he must prevent 1 from dribbling back to the middle.

A teammate of X2 can shoot the gap on 2 for an interception. This teammate must leave as X2 begins his run. Other defenders who wish to shoot other gaps must also depart as X2 embarks. There can be no hesitations.

1's second choice would be a pass into the area just vacated by the gap shooter on 2. Because of the distance of these two passes and the unsure behavior of 1, these passes will often be intercepted, especially when the long run and jump is used after the other stunts have made 1 hesitant to throw the obvious pass. Even when the pass is completed, the new rotating defenders can stop further penetration (see Chapter 1).

The long run and jump trap can be employed after the offensive team has successfully cleared out; or it can cause havoc with teams that like to attack using only two widely spread guards. Because 1 sees only defenders and those at a great distance from him, it is difficult for the dribbler to find an open teammate.

GIVE THE OUTSIDE, THEN TAKE IT AWAY

X1, in Diagram 2-11, originally lines up as if he is calling the long run and jump. X2, however, cannot run and jump because 2 might have located too near the scoring area. Or, there might be no attacker and therefore no defender in the sideline area. In this case X1 must race back hard to a recovery position on 1, forcing him to change his direction. When X3 sees X1 beginning to take the outside away from 1, X3 comes over to double-team with X1. X3 should surprise 1 just as 1 completes his reverse dribble. A defender shooting the gap on 3 would get a lay-up if 1 makes the obvious pass.

SUMMARY OF TRAPS

We trap motionless attackers (blitz trap). We trap them when they dribble toward us (jump trap, run and jump trap, long run and jump trap). We start a trap in one direction, then trap in another (give the outside, then take it away). We trap after a defensive fake (hedging followed by a trap). We can combine them (Diagram 2-11 shows X2 hedging while X1 and X3 eventually set the trap).

The two players involved in trapping must recognize situations developing. The other three defenders must perceive the trap developing and respond by covering their men and the passing lanes near their men. None of these defenders may hesitate. When they begin moving, they must race hard. Gap shooters begin when they see the trapper's first step.

These traps, where passing lanes are covered, coupled with the switches (developed next), where each man is individually covered, can thoroughly confuse the dribbler. Add the team techniques of later chapters and the best offensive teams will have trouble weaving their way out of our defensive web.

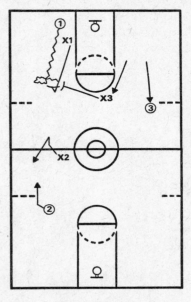

Diagram 2-11

DOUBLE-TEAMING AND SHOOTING THE GAPS

All players must know how to double-team (Diagram 2-3). Defenders must also know how to shoot the gaps for steals (Diagram 2-12). They must understand when to begin their move toward a gap. The following drill not only teaches how and when, but it provides the repetition needed to make the moves instinctive.

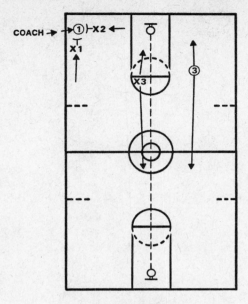

Diagram 2-12

Defensive drills should not exist unless they are an integral part of the team defense. This drill will be seen many times in many forms as a part of other drills. It should be introduced early in the master practice schedule so that the other drills can be added to it (for example, Chapter 1, Diagram 1-11).

Procedure (Diagram 2-12):

1. Line players up in one line. Rotate from 1 to X1 to X2 to 3 to X3 to end of the line.
2. Coach passes to 1 to activate the drill.
3. 1 does not have a dribble, or the drill at this stage can be run like the double-teaming drill (Diagram 2-3) with X1 and X2 stopping the dribble.
4. X1 and X2 double-team 1.
5. X3 stays within interception distance of 3, but not up against him.
6. 3 can move up and down the court but does not come across a half-court imaginary line (dotted).

7. After the double-team, 1 tries to pass to 3 and X3 tries to
   intercept. 1 must not lob pass.

Objectives:

1. To teach defenders how to shoot the gap and steal a pass.
2. To teach 1 how to pass under double-team pressure.
3. To teach double-teams the proper method of forcing a
   bad pass in order to help X3 pick it off.
4. To teach X3 the perfect position from which to shoot the
   gap for a steal.

HOW TO SWITCH OUT OF AN UNSUCCESSFUL TRAP

Trappers call traps by yelling "trap." "Jump" would call a
switch. "Used" called by the trapper tells the container to leave
the trap and find the open man. When a pass is made out of the
trap, the container leaves to find the open man. The trapper
stays with the passer, but he must race upfloor, relocating above
the ball. Neither the trapper nor the container watches the flight
of the pass. Both leave immediately.

While the trapper merely reestablishes his position in relation to the ball and his man, the container must rotate to an open
attacker. The container revolves (fish hooks) back in the direction from which the trapper came (Diagram 2-13). The container
first checks the defensive coverage on the trapper's ex-man. If
the trapper's ex-man is not covered, he is now the container's

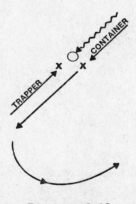

Diagram 2-13

new man (a simple switch between the trapper and the container). If the trapper's ex-man is blanketed, the container circles until he finds the open man. This circuit takes the container toward the defensive basket and then back out.

HOW TO SWITCH

"Jump" calls an immediate switch. "Used" calls a switch after the dribbler has picked up his dribble, usually after a trap. "Switch" is used by two defenders away from the ball in back court or by two defenders on the ball in front court. When "jump" or "used" is signalled by the trapper, the container rotates as described in the section above. In the back court situation the defender moving away from the ball calls "switch," and that defender becomes responsible for the attacker moving toward the ball. In the front court the defender off the ball calls "switch" and rotates to the ball.

When a trapper calls "jump" or "used," he keeps his body in the obvious passing lane, attempting to deflect any pass into that lane. The container must race hard to get into the obvious passing lane when he hears his cue to switch. The container should intercept any pass thrown there.

JUMP SWITCH

After jump-trapping successfully a few times, our defenders may introduce the jump switch. Its mechanics are the same as the jump trap, except the trappers yell "jump." "Jump" tickets the container to switch.

In Diagram 2-6, X2 would jump at least one step and a long jump into the dribbling lane of 1. When X2 yells "jump," X1 must react by getting between 1 and 2, guarding 2.

1, who may have reversed into traps previously, possibly charged, or had the ball stolen by X1, will pick up his dribble. With the ball in his hand and all the attackers covered individually, 1 may be unable to pass the ball without it being deflected or stolen. X2 must pressure 1, preventing him from finding any temporarily open attacker. If 1 loops out of the switch, X2 defends him one-on-one until another teammate institutes another stunt.

BLITZ SWITCH

"Jump" signals this switch (Diagram 2-14). 1 has not dribbled, waiting for the clearout of his teammates. When 1 sees X1 leave, he may decide to dribble down the sideline (if it appears open). Another defensive teammate, located downcourt in the sideline lane, can activiate the long run and jump switch or trap. Or X2 can use the give-the-outside-then-take-it-away switch or trap.

1 may not take the bait. He could still wait until all is cleared out. X1 could then come back and blitz trap, or he could follow 2 downcourt. 1 would merely have wasted more of his precious ten seconds. He must dribble or pass. If each defender covers his man, he cannot pass. When he dribbles, another stunt awaits him.

RUN AND JUMP SWITCH

X2, in Diagram 2-15, must be within 20 feet and 1 must be dribbling toward X2 before X2 can initiate a run and jump. X1 must stay with 1 until X2 has 1 under control. X1 must prevent 1 from dribbling back toward the middle until he abandons 1 for X2 to cover. When X1 leaves, he must get in the passing lane between 1 and 2.

X2 should race at the shoulder of 1's dribbling hand. This prohibits 1 from advancing with his dribble, and it compels him to either pick up his dribble or change his direction. 1 will hesitate to change his direction, especially if he has previously experienced a run and jump trap. He cannot be sure if the defense intends the run and jump trap or the run and jump switch, and therefore will probably pick up his dribble.

All gap shooters must leave their assigned men to shoot the gap at the exact moment X2 leaves his man to commence the run and jump trap or switch. Any gap shooter who delays, even momentarily, should stay with his appointed man.

Run and jump switches and traps work best after a dribbling reverse. Dribblers have no view of their receivers after a reverse. That gives the trapper a bigger element of surprise, and it gives his teammates longer time to rotate.

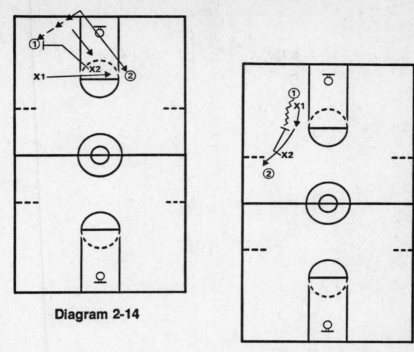

Diagram 2-14

Diagram 2-15

LONG RUN AND JUMP SWITCH

X2 races toward 1 in the passing lane (Diagram 2-16). X1 departs immediately upon hearing "jump" to get in the obvious passing lane. But if X2 hollers "trap," X1 stays.

Long run and jump switches are used infrequently. They serve to keep the attackers off-balance and guessing. Occasionally, 1 will pick up his dribble or throw a hurried pass toward the obvious pass receiver, 2, and X1 can pick up an interception.

Clearouts offer the best opportunity to force a ten-second violation with the long run and jump. 1 waits a few seconds for his teammates to clear the back court. X1 directs 1 down the outside lane, every dribble taking another second. X2 races directly at 1's dribbling shoulder, yelling "jump." 1 dribble-loops as X2 contains. Another defender from the middle lane area begins a run and jump trap. 1 may not find a receiver before the allotted ten count.

Diagram 2-16

SUMMARY OF SWITCHES

Switches and traps, when combined intelligently, offer an unsurmountable obstacle for an attacking team to hurdle, especially when applied for the duration of a game. Many teams spend their practice sessions preparing for the presses, hurting their half-court attack.

Defensive teams can switch out of any trapping situation ("jump" or "trap"). They can even switch after applying the trap and forcing the dribbler to pick up the ball ("used"). Giving-the-outside-then-taking-it-away can be switched or trapped. And switching should occur when any dribbler follows a reverse by picking up his dribble. Hedging can precede a switch.

A ROTATION DRILL
TO DETERMINE WHO SWITCHES TO WHOM

Coaches cannot expect players to react instinctively to maneuvers which have only been talked about. Players must be drilled and drilled and drilled again. After hours of determined drilling the maneuvers may become a reflex action.

The following is a rotation drill involving two defenders against one ball handler. More drills dealing with proper rotation will be given in Chapter 7. These drills are not presented here because of their importance to developing the run and jump team defense described in Chapter 7.

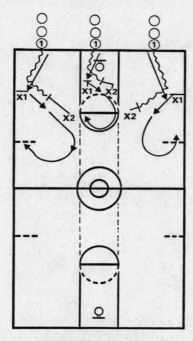

Diagram 2-17

Procedure (Diagram 2-17):

1. Line players up as shown. Rotate from 1 to X1 to X2 to the end of the line after completing a trip downfloor and back.
2. 1 attacks down the floor and back. X1 and X2 defend. 1 cannot dribble out of his lane.
3. X2 can yell "jump," which will force X1 to run the "fish hook" looking for his open man. X2 can yell "trap," forcing X1 to help trap; X2 can follow "trap" with "used,"

again sending X1 to find the open attacker (fish hook route). After "used," 1 must wait three seconds before he can begin dribbling again. This would allow X1 time to run his route and recover.

4. X2 would cut 1 toward X1, and X1 would run at 1 yelling "trap," "jump," or "used" during the second phase. The third phase would reoccur as in Step 3, the fourth phase would be a repetition of Step 4, and so on.

Objectives:

1. To teach communication.
2. To teach proper and instant rotation.
3. To teach continuous "jump," "used," and "trap" reactions.
4. To teach techniques of run and jumping, double-teaming, and leaving the attacker who has lost his dribble.

RUN AND NO-JUMP STRATEGY

During the course of a season, there will be offensive players who the defensive coach will not want to handle the ball in the front court. Such players are usually great penetrators and passers or great scorers. Keeping the ball away from such players might bring victory.

The defensive coach might have one particular defender that he wants covering that great penetrator. When that situation develops, the coach would want to employ the run and no-jump strategy. It can only be called by the coach, and it must be pre-planned and pre-practiced.

For the sake of discussion, let's have 1 represent a great penetrator (Diagram 2-18). X2, any defensive helper of X1, activates the run and jump trap or the blitz trap. No signal is used; no words uttered. When 1 picks up the dribble, X2 runs the fish hook, searching for the open man (usually his assigned man).

Because 1 is the opposition's most dangerous passer, we ordinarily do not employ any gap shooting. After 1 passes the ball, X1 prevents him from receiving it back. Should 1 receive the ball back, another defender traps (run and jump or blitz)

with X1 until 1 passes. Hence, the process of preventing a pass
to 1 begins again.

   We prefer to prevent 1 from crossing the time line dribbling the basketball. This compels our opposition to attack us
with at least their second best playmaker. And, the defense
looses nothing in trying.

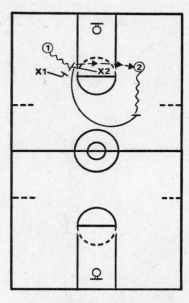

Diagram 2-18

3

Preventing
the In-Bounds Pass

After we score, an opponent must take the ball out-of-bounds and pass it to one of his teammates. This begins their attack. Stopping this throw-in becomes our first line of defense. We have a variety of methods for preventing the completion of this in-bounds pass. This chapter presents those defensive maneuvers.

Once the ball is in-bounded successfully, we employ the individual techniques of Chapters 2 and 4 or the team techniques of Chapters 6, 7, and 8 to prevent the ball from being advanced to front court. When a team does maneuver the ball into front court, we initiate our half-court pressure man-to-man defense.

PLAYING THE OUT-OF-BOUNDS PASSER

An out-of-bounds passer is the first attacker that the defense sees. Pressuring that passer's view will prevent him from quickly spotting an open in-bounds receiver. Deflecting his pass often leads to a defensive recovery, followed by an easy, quick basket. Because we can accomplish these two objectives more efficiently with a man-to-man press, we frequently try to dominate the out-of-bounds passer.

However, the out-of-bounds passer's defender can, at his discretion or at the beckon of his coach, drop to the free throw circle and play the lobbed in-bounds pass. He frequently does this when his teammates are face-guarding the in-bounds receivers (see later sections in this chapter).

An effective offensive maneuver against point zone presses allows one player to take the ball out-of-bounds and pass to another player who also locates out-of-bounds. This relieves the defensive pressure on the out-of-bounds passer. But this cannot gain an advantage against man-to-man presses, since the second out-of-bounds passer would still be covered by his assigned defender.

Unlike the zone defenders, who have only one specific player assigned to the out-of-bounds passer, all man-to-man defenders must know how to cover the out-of-bounds attacker. If the throw-in occurs after a violation, the passer cannot run the baseline without walking, making it easier for the defender to influence the out-of-bounds passer. If the throw-in follows a successful score, the out-of-bounds passer can run the baseline, impelling the defender to defensively slide to keep his position.

This defender should keep his eyes on the passer's eyes and feet. The out-of-bounds passer usually looks where he will throw the ball. His feet will indicate the distance he intends to throw it: parallel feet mean a short, quick in-bounds pass and staggered feet forecast a long pass. The ball held overhead predicts a lob pass, maintained at chest level indicates the bounce pass, and balanced with one hand beside the ear foretells a baseball pass. The defender's arms should wave frantically in a windmill fashion over the strong shoulder (right for right-handed dribblers, left for left-handed passers) of the passer if the defender suspects the long pass. The long pass is usually thrown with one hand. If the defender sees parallel feet or if the opposition attacks with the short passing game, this defender should wave his arms from a 45° angle above his shoulder to his waist. This impels the lob or bounce pass, both easily intercepted passes. He should also constantly throw his leg out in the direction he expects the pass. Such deflections, although creating a violation, will cause the attacker to be a little more hesitant with his next pass, making it easier to intercept. The defender should watch the passer's body. The passer usually steps in the direction he bounce-passes. Defenders should place their bodies directly in the bounce-passing lane.

Defenders on the out-of-bounds passer must also yell. This

not only disconcerts the passer, but it permits the face-guarding in-bounds defenders (see a later section in this chapter) to know where the running baseline passer locates and relocates. This is especially important when our in-bounds defenders are switching from face-guard to denial to face-guard, and so on.

Defenders on out-of-bounds passers should strive to keep their bodies in a direct line with the passer and the area where a screen is about to occur. Scouting reports might tip the defenders as to where to expect a screen. But when facing an unknown or highly versatile offense, the defender should shade to the inside. It is slower to pass to the outside, and there is much less area for the in-bounds receiver to operate. Defenders on in-bounds receivers also have better angles for intercepting passes thrown to the outside. And should the pass be completed, teammates can institute better defensive stunts in the outside lanes and they can halt a breakaway dribbler more easily. But if the out-of-bounds passer locates directly underneath the backboard, his defender should drop four feet back, getting directly underneath his basket with his hands revolving between knee level and shoulder level. Only a bounce pass or a chest pass can be thrown. Anything higher would hit the back of the backboard, constituting a violation. Anything low should be deflected or stolen.

Tight or loose coverage on this out-of-bounds passer offers equal success. Alternating these coverages can confuse the passer into making even more mistakes. Basically, loose coverage should be used when the passer tips his passing angle, and tight coverage should unnerve an unpoised passer. When the in-bounds defender is very quick with his hands or legs, loose coverage will permit him to deflect or steal many slow in-bounds passes. Loose coverage, however, should never exceed three or four feet.

DOUBLE ON THE OUT-OF-BOUNDS PASSER

Many offensive coaches do not believe in the long pass from out-of-bounds. They find it uncontrollable, especially in high school. Such coaches counter pressure defenses with a short passing game. When we face this short passing attack, we frequently double on the out-of-bounds passer.

Out-of-bounds passers have only three short passing lanes:

diagonally to their right, down the middle, and diagonally to their left. A defender covering the left lane and a defender stationed in the right lane concedes only the middle lane. When these two defenders concentrate on that middle lane with their arms and legs, they can deflect many bounce and chest passes directed there. Only lob passes over these defenders (and we usually use our two biggest defenders here) or bounce passes around them can be successful. Proper denial or face-guard pressure on the first two attackers should result in an interception.

Doubling on the out-of-bounds passer also works well against the long passing attack. Defenders are already located on both of the attacker's shoulders. When expecting the long pass, the defenders raise their arms above their heads and wave frantically. This forces a higher lob. When expecting the short pass, the arms should windmill between the waist and a 45° angle above the shoulder.

When a team is down by four or less points with about ten seconds left, they can tie or regain the lead by scoring and quickly double-teaming the out-of-bounds passer with their two tallest defenders. In fact, this strategy can be used at different intervals during the game, not just the last defensive play. When this tactic is used infrequently, it often results in a five-second in-bounding violation against both the long and the short passing attacks. Such manipulations must be called from the bench.

MAKE WEAK BALL HANDLERS HANDLE THE BALL

Playing defense behind the weak ball handler while face-guarding the skilled dribbler, and pressuring the side of the out-of-bounds passer that coincides with the location of the clever ball handler, leaves an open passing lane to the weak ball handler. The out-of-bounds passer, under the pressure of a ball game, will often pass to that open lane (line of least resistance). Once the ball is in-bounded to this weak ball handler (passer and/or dribbler), we can begin one of the harassing stunts described in this book to compel this weak attacker to turn over the ball. For example: If he were a weak passer from a stationary position, we would blitz trap; if he were a poor passer off the dribble, we would force the dribble by covering all passing lanes and run and jump when the dribble began.

PLAYING THE IN-BOUNDS RECEIVER

In-bounds receivers have four basic cuts in relation to the out-of-bounds passer: the vertical cut, the horizontal cut, the deep cut, and the diagonal cut (Diagram 3-1). Fakes usually precede the actual cut, but most players have a favorite maneuver that they couple with their pet fakes. To these individual cuts, offensive teams add certain screening maneuvers. Or, they may combine the cuts and screening maneuvers in any commutative (doubles) or associative (triples) order.

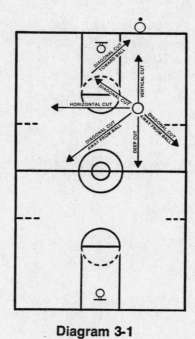

Diagram 3-1

Anytime a cutter breaks to a side lane, his defender should body-check any attempt by that cutter to get back to the center lane. Defenders can accomplish this with denial or face-guard pressure.

Allowing the in-bounds pass, then containing the dribbler before activating a gambling stunt offers one method of guarding the in-bounds receiver. Face-guarding, thereby forcing the downcourt lob pass, presents a second alternative. And, denying with a closed denial stance advances a third means of playing the in-bounds receiver. Each maneuver used by the attacking team will be analyzed and countered in the following sections.

The vertical cut. An in-bounds attacker breaking directly toward the out-of-bounds passer uses the vertical cut. Unless a defender stops this cutter's progress, an open in-bounding passing lane results. We prefer for our defender to step (getting both feet on the floor prior to contact) in front of the vertical cutter, facing him. Continued offensive movement would terminate in a charge. The vertical cutter must stop and veer in a horizontal or diagonal direction. Usually, this change of direction follows a fake in the opposite direction. So we do not honor the first step from a vertical to a new direction. On the second step we change from face-guard to denial with an arm, head, and a foot between the passer and the receiver. If the vertical cutter continues in that direction, we should steal the slow bounce pass. If he used the first two steps as a fake to change directions, he would on his first step back have placed his body in a line with our body and the passer. That would again represent face-guarding. His second step, which would be his first step away from our body, would not be honored. His second step away from our body, his third step after changing directions, would reactivate our denial stance.

Vertical cutters sometimes go to screen down on another defender. When played properly, this cannot be successful (see sections on screening).

The horizontal cut. Horizontal cutters move away from the passer, offering the defense the best angle to intercept any pass directed toward the horizontal cutter. The horizontal cutters' greatest threats are their screening angles to help a teammate get open and their ensuing perfect positioning, after screening and rolling, to diagonally cut back toward the ball. Screening is discussed last in this section.

As a cutter moves at a 90° angle away from the ball, his

defender moves away from him toward the ball, but at such an angle that he can deflect any chest pass thrown toward the horizontal cutter. This prevents the quick change of direction with a diagonal cut back toward the ball. This man's defender would simply step (both feet on floor prior to contact) in front of the diagonal cutter and draw the charge. Usually, this horizontal cutter will wave to the passer for a lob pass, which can be deflected or intercepted. Or, he will break on a deep cut or a deep diagonal cut away from the ball.

The deep cut. Any movement downfloor away from the out-of-bounds passer represents the deep cut. Because it is movement away from the ball, we drop off this attacker after we have sighted the passer. We first want to sight the passer to see if he is throwing long before we allow daylight between us and the deep cutter. This drop also eliminates an attacking teammate from using a deep cutter's screen to get open. This drop also gives the deep cutter's defender a little more time to "switch" to the attacker using the screen. This drop conforms to our principle of sagging and floating: staying two-thirds the distance from the ball to our man.

The diagonal cut. Diagonal cutters, unless properly resisted, can solve the difficulties of in-bounding the ball against a good press, man-to-man or zone. When the diagonal cutter moves away from the ball, although lessening his vertical distance from it (cut 1 in Diagram 3-2), his defender must play denial defense. This defender must never locate less than an arm's distance off the direct line between the passer and the cutter. This prevents a chest pass to this cutter. The defender must be able to see both his man and the ball. Should the diagonal cutter break diagonally back toward the ball, his defender must step in front of this cut, drawing the charge if the cutter continues. Once a diagonal cutter breaks into either outside lane, his defender must never let him maneuver back into the middle lane. He has restricted his receiving area, and we want to keep it confined.

Diagonal cutters moving away from the ball and lengthening their vertical distance can receive only the lob pass, as in the deep cut (cut 3 in Diagram 3-2). Their defenders must first check

the passer to see if the lob is forthcoming before dropping and
floating. When the offense does not use the lob pass, this defender locates two-thirds the distance from the ball to his man and
one step off the line between the passer and his man for every 20
feet his man is away from the ball.

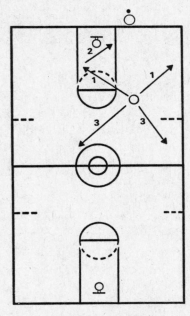

Diagram 3-2

The diagonal cutter has the best screening angle. However,
we initially locate in a position to prevent the diagonal cutter
from moving toward the screen (see next section).

The screening maneuvers. Our defensive rule when facing
screeners—prevent the screener from setting the screen—puts
the defense on the offensive. But situations do exist which prevent the application of this rule, deep cut screeners for example
(Diagram 3-3). When this happens, we want the quick jump
switch into the running lane of the man receiving the screen by
the original screener's defender. The original screener's defender must yell "switch" as he jumps into the passing lane
between the passer and the cutter. The switcher must get into

the running lane with both feet on the floor prior to contact. This requires concentration and repetitive drilling, basic characteristics of all championship teams.

Diagram 3-3 shows 1 racing to screen X2. X2 will blast hard into 1's pick if 1 does not allow him at least one full step. An illegal screening foul on 1 would result. If 1 allows the required step, X2 must recover into denial position on 1. He can do this because X1 has told him to "watch the screen" and "switch." If 1 has an opening on his cut back to the ball, it is at the moment of the screen. But X3 is aware of this and should prevent any pass except the lob, which X2 should deflect. X1 would switch to 2, playing denial or face-guard (see later section this chapter). When 1 breaks back toward 3, he will usually use the diagonal cut. X2 should be aware of this, and he should play the proper angle to intercept the slow bounce pass.

Diagram 3-4 depicts the horizontal screener. X2 will have sagged toward the ball, using the backboard to prevent the lob pass and his arms to prevent the chest pass, allowing only the

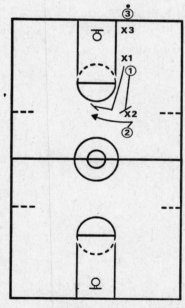

Diagram 3-3

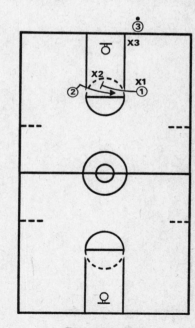

Diagram 3-4

slow bounce pass. This forces 1 to screen down a small distance.
Should 2 begin his cut prior to 1's screen and 1 not stop completely before setting the screen, X2 blasts through the screen,
compelling the official to call the illegal screen. X1 will also be
playing denial defense on 1. When X1 suspects that 1 intends to
set a horizontal screen, he should step in front of 1 if possible,
drawing the charge as 1 continues. But should X1 be unable to
prevent the screen, he must be prepared to "jump switch" into
2's path as 2 cuts around 1's screen. X2 switches to 1 as 1 diagonally cuts toward the passer, 3. X3 has heard the conversation,
"watch the screen" and "switch," so he should know the area of
the screen. X3 must help X2 and X1 by placing his body in the
passing lane between the passer and the point where the screen
was set. This helps prevent the direct pass in-bounds, should
either 1 or 2 be open temporarily.

Diagrams 3-5 and 3-6 illustrate the diagonal screens. 2, in
Diagram 3-5, could screen up on X1, or 1 could screen down on
X2. Neither should achieve much success for they must veer
their direct screening routes because their defenders would

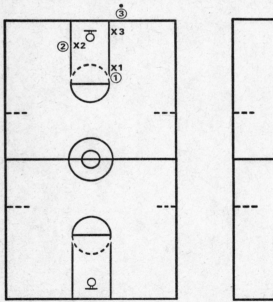

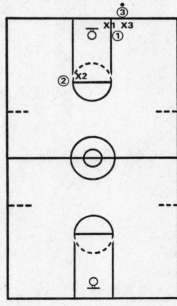

Diagram 3-5   Diagram 3-6

draw a charge on any straight cut. X3 can help the screened defenders by placing his body between the passer and the area where he hears the command, "watch the screen." A successful screen by either 1 or 2 would meet resistance in a defensive jump switch. "Switch" would be the command. Such a switch would prevent the cutter from being open. And the screener would probably roll to the ball. But the screener's new defender, with a quick half-step, can easily regain denial position.

The diagonal screeners in Diagram 3-6 offer more challenging defensive problems. Here, the screen is at an angle away from the ball (1 going to screen X2). X1 had to play 1 with either face-guard or denial, eliminating positioning between 1 and X2. However, X1 can drop off 1 as he sets the screen, and X1 can quickly switch to 2. A lob pass to 2 might prove successful. But when 1 rolls back toward the ball, he would have X2 on his back. 1 would momentarily be open. X3 must place his body in this passing lane, forcing the semi-lob which X2 can deflect. Should 2 move to use 1's screen before 1 completely stops, we want X2 blasting into 1 for the illegal screen turnover. X1 can cue X2 with "slide," demanding X2 to stay with 2.

A screen down by 2 on X1 in Diagram 3-6 is not nearly as successful an offensive move. X2, playing denial, forces 2 to alter his screening route or charge. Hence, a successful screen would result with X2 between the ball and 1 and X1 between the ball and 2.

Diagram 3-7 represents parallel screeners. X2 stations himself in the gap between 1 and 2 while X1 locates on the ball-side shoulder of 1. X3 puts his body in the passing lane from the passer to the spot of the intended screen. Should 3 run the baseline, X3 would be yelling, disconcerting the passer and telling X2 and X1 to relocate. The defender away from the ball would line up in the gap and the defender nearest the ball aligns himself on the ball-side shoulder of the nearest receiver. Denial defense is played. Any screening maneuver would be jump switched. Such a defense would still have a defender between the attacker and the ball.

Tandem screeners (Diagram 3-8), when played properly, cannot solve a good press. X2 stations himself exactly parallel to and on the ball side of 1. X1 plays half-a-man to the ball side of 1.

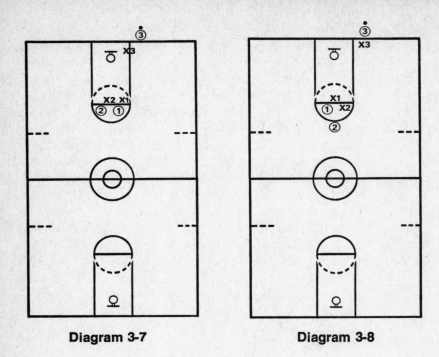

Diagram 3-7   **Diagram 3-8**

If 1 screened for 2, X1 and X2 would jump switch, keeping their denial positioning on 2 and 1 respectively. 2 cannot screen 1 except for a deep cut. A jump switch on this maneuver would result in the defenders still being in denial positioning. 2 might cut deep on an individual cut, but X2's positioning would permit him to go with 2. 2 might dip toward X2 and cut off 1, using 1 as a screener. However, X1 would have time to read such a cut and jump switch into the passing lane between 3 and 2. X2 would take a half-step toward the ball into perfect denial positioning on 1. It would also represent the same placement that was evident in the parallel screening maneuvers (Diagram 3-7). Only a defensive mistake can help the tandem screeners get open. X3 helps by placing his body in the passing lane between 3 and the area of the proposed screen. X1 and X2 would adjust their positioning if 3 races along the baseline. X3 would communicate this to X1 and X2.

The doubles and the triples. Doubles means that an attacker has used two of the above cuts and/or screens in rapid order. A triple would indicate that three such offensive maneuvers have occurred, one following another. There isn't time to use four (a five-second violation). We have also observed: When a cutter does not get open immediately, he has a tendency to break back toward the passer. So if a cutter cannot free himself within three seconds, his defender should expect him to come back toward the ball.

Doubles and triples are defended by repeating our techniques in the same rapid order that the offense makes use of their maneuvers. Defenders must drill on all commutative (doubles) and associative (triples) orders. Usually, the next scheduled team has favorite combinations. Scouting will tell the coach those mixtures. By year's end, the team should have faced all possible combinations. They should be well prepared for the tournament trail.

FACE-GUARD

Face-guarding defenders do not see the passer. They only see their assigned men. Because of this, face-guarders must read the expressions on their attacker's face. They must guess when the lob pass will come over their head, and they should jump to deflect it. Defenders on the out-of-bounds passer can tell the in-bounds defender of the oncoming pass. Defenders on the out-of-bounds passer must disrupt this passer's concentration.

Face-guarding has its value in full court pressure schemes. There are those attackers who cannot stand the constant harassment. Some out-of-bounds passers will not throw the ball in-bounds unless they can see the in-bounds receiver clearly; and against face-guard pressure, the in-bounds receiver's defender will always be between his man and the ball. Many attackers, when faced with a face-guard, will cut on a deep route, permitting a deeper defender to draw a charge. Face-guarding, used discreetly, can force a five-second violation.

When we prevent the pass in-bounds, we like to play part face-guard, part denial. We face-guard attackers who are vertical to the passer. When those vertical attackers take one step, we ignore it. When they take a second step in that same direction, we go to denial.

DENIAL

Denying the in-bounds pass can lead to an offensive turn-over which will result in a quick, demoralizing lay-up. We play denial on all players diagonal to the passer. Each step taken away from the denial defender is covered by a slide step; but the first two steps taken toward the denial defender are covered by swinging from denial to face-guard to denial on the opposite side. The first step puts the attacker behind the defender's body. The second step would find the defender's opposite foot and arm between the attacker and the ball.

If the denial defender is on the side away from the ball, he can use the backboard to force the bounce pass (Diagram 3-9). A lob pass cannot be thrown into the shaded area without hitting the back of the backboard. A direct chest pass should be deflected by the out-of-bound's defender. Therefore, the bounce pass will be used. A smart defender, on the side away from the ball, can play a step farther off the line between the passer and his attacker. The out-of-bounds passer will think this in-bounds receiver open and direct a bounce pass to him. The bounce pass is slow, and the defender who intercepts it has an uncontested two points.

Our denial defense is a fence step. We have an arm, a leg, and a head between the passer and our assigned man. The first step forward is taken by the denial foot. The trailing foot is then brought up to the heel of the denial foot.

Procedure (Diagram 3-10):

1. Players are to get down in normal fencing position—feet at right angles, hands out front as if they are holding a foil.
2. Players are to use fence slides as though they are attacking.
3. On visual command, the coach has the players advance, retreat, advance, retreat, until they go the full length of the court. Start the drill slowly then build up speed.
4. Coach must be careful that players keep their body balance (weight evenly distributed), and that their feet do not slide along the floor but are raised very slightly.

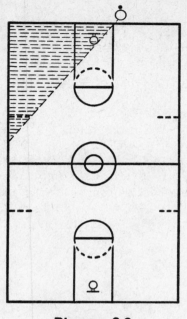

Diagram 3-9   **Diagram 3-10**

Objectives:

1. To condition legs in normal guarding position.
2. To teach defensive movement that must be used to deny in-bounds passes, vertical passes, and passes into the middle lane.
3. To teach visual reaction and concentration.
4. To develop quickness of the feet.

THE CENTER FIELD

The terms "center field," "short stop," and "left field," used first by Morgan Wootten at DeMatha High School, were borrowed from baseball. They describe the initial location of X3, the defender on the out-of-bounds passer. Each has a different starting location, and each is run for different reasons.

Center field strategy operates as a counter to the successful completion of lob passes to 1 or 2 (Diagram 3-11). The center fielder can also gravitate toward the area where 1 and 2 have operated successful screening maneuvers. By playing a center fielder, X1 and X2 can exaggerate their face-guarding or their denials, knowing that X3 can compensate.

Center fielders, on the first few possessions, should locate at the head of the circle unless the defensive coach is using this method as a defensive counter to the successful lobs and screens. Then, the center fielder would locate in the area needed. By showing this new variation, offensive teams must adjust to different and more dangerous maneuvers, often without having practiced them. Successful in-bounded passes to either 1 or 2 can still be trapped or switched (see Chapter 2). Should the ball be in-bounded to either 1 or 2 and no switch or trap was offered, X3 would pick up 3. But if X3 tried to intercept a lob, he could require either X1 or X2 to switch to 3 by the word "jump."

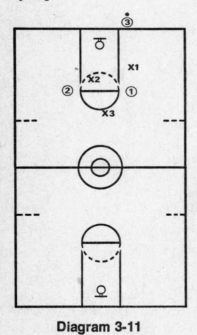

Diagram 3-11

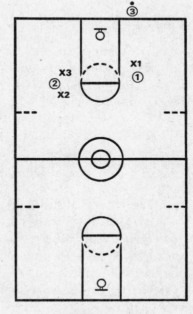

Diagram 3-12

THE SHORT STOP

Short-stopping prevents an in-bounds pass to a particular receiver, 2 in Diagram 3-12. The short stop, X3, the defender who originally covered the out-of-bounds passer, locates in front of and face-guards 2. 2's appointed defender drops behind and to the ball side of 2. X2 and X3 double-team 2, preventing the pass to him.

Teams that attack full court man-to-man pressure with only one guard, 2, can be forced to bring down a helper by the short stop, illustrating the defense forcing the offense to make another adjustment. After this offensive adjustment the defense can still commence its traps, switches, three-man stunts, etc., forcing even greater and more dangerous offensive adjustments (see Chapters 2 and 6).

Teams that run patterned attacks and have one man assigned to receive the in-bounds pass fall easy prey to the short-stopping maneuver. By keeping that player from receiving the ball, the offense must make unpracticed adjustments which will lead to total chaos.

Many teams have one exceptional ball handler and penetrator. To deny this ball handler the ball would force the offense to operate with its second-best quarterback. When we call the run and no-jump strategy (see Chapter 2), we begin with double coverage (short-stopping) on the in-bounds receiver we do not want handling the ball.

X3 would cover 3 in the event 3 can successfully in-bounds the ball. Then X1, X2, and X3 could run any stunt to prevent further advancement of the ball.

THE LEFT FIELD

Left fielders line up at the opposite free throw line. They can prevent any long lob pass. They are an added safety; they will not allow a lay-up.

All the other defenders can exaggerate their denial and face-guard defense because they know they have a teammate (the left fielder—X3 in Diagram 3-13) who will cover for them. We use their strategy late in a game which we are winning because it prevents the offense from getting the easy shot and yet permits us to continue pressure, possibly forcing a bad in-bounds pass. This strategy is also excellent against teams that like deep cutters (from which we can draw the charge) or teams that like to long-lob or baseball-pass (from which we can steal the pass).

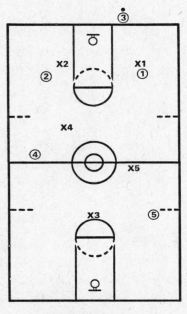

Diagram 3-13

However, a completed pass to 1 or 2 would break the press. 1 or 2 would simply pass back to 3 who could bring the ball downcourt uncontested.

X3 would cover 3 around midcourt, unless he jumped on a cutter where the ball was involved or switched on a screen where the ball was not involved (see Chapter 2). Then, the defender that X3 called off would cover 3.

ANALYZING AND DEFENDING
DIFFERENT METHODS OF IN-BOUNDING THE BALL

Telling players how to defend, giving them the savvy, is not enough. Players learn only by doing. So if a number of different drills are offered, they will not get stale, regardless of the length of the season or the length of the daily practice schedule. Coaches cannot see five-on-five as clearly as they can see three-on-three or less. So we use as many drills as we can with a small number of players confined to a small area. It expedites our teaching and their learning. It enables us to see and to correct all mistakes.

Several drills are used to inculcate into our players the ideas of this chapter. Defenders go over and over these drills until their moves become instinctive. We begin with our version of the cutthroat drill (Diagram 3-14), advancing to what we call our 3, 4, 5, and 6 drills defensively.

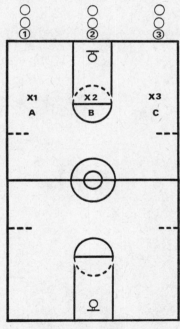

Diagram 3-14

Procedure (Diagram 3-14):

1. Line players up as shown in groups of three.
2. A, B, and C begin the drill by attacking X1, X2, and X3.
3. If A, B, and C score, they immediately take the ball out-of-bounds. We usually have the player in the center

line take the ball out-of-bounds. He is to pass it in-bounds to either of his two teammates. These three immediately attack the goal again. Because A, B, and C scored, X1, X2, and X3 go to the end of the line. 1, 2, and 3 race onto the floor, ready to deny the in-bounds pass from B to either A or C. The coach can specify which cut or screening maneuver (usually the maneuver used by the next opponent) he wants used. He may also call for 2, X2, or B to use short-stopping, left field, or center field techniques.

4. If A, B, or C miss and X1, X2, or X3 get the defensive rebound, then X2 would take the ball out-of-bounds and pass it to X1 or X3. Again, 1, 2, and 3 would have to hurry onto the court into denial position on X1, X2, and X3. The coach can assign cuts, screens, and defensive movements he wants the offense or the defense to use.

5. As the season progresses we use the three-on-three drill over the entire court. By placing three men out-of-bounds on each end line, we have a continuous three-on-three full court game. But we change the rules slightly. The team that scores stays on defense. The three out-of-bounds men become the new offense.

6. When we switch to full court, we require the attackers to receive the in-bounds pass below the free throw line, and all offensive players must remain below the advancement of the ball. This gives us no offensive clear-outs, enabling us to work on any or all of our defensive three-man stunts.

Objectives:

1. To teach a small number of players in a smaller area so that the coach can more quickly see and correct mistakes.

2. To teach defenders all the techniques of this chapter. To teach attackers how to attack a press.

3. To require defenders to quickly pick up their men as they would have to do during a game.

4. To teach our three-on-three defensive stunts.

5. To condition players to play the full court defensive game.

6. To develop instinctive defensive reactions.
7. To develop aggressive defenders.

The Three Drill Offensively

Procedure (Diagram 3-15):

1. Line players up as shown. The first three players in the
   line activate the three drill: 1 drives the length of the
   floor for a lay-up; 2 lets 1 reach the foul line, 15 feet
   away, and then tries to catch him before he can drive the
   remaining 75 feet and lay the ball in; 3 races downcourt to
   guard 1 as he tries to receive the throw-in.
2. After 1's lay-up, 2 takes the ball out-of-bounds, 3 guards

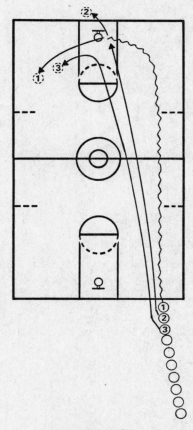

Diagram 3-15

1 (face-guard, denial, slough or whatever the coach
wants) while 2 tries to pass the ball in-bounds.
3. If 3 face-guards 1, then 1 must receive the in-bounds
pass below the free throw line. This situation simulates
having a deeper defender to steal any lob pass.
4. When ball is in-bounded, 1 and 2 fast-break while 3
defends.
5. The second group of three players begins their drill
when the first group reaches midcourt on their return
trip.

Objectives:
1. To teach 2 to catch 1 and block the shot or foul, preventing the easy lay-up.
2. To teach 2 to pass in-bounds against pressure or denial
defense, and to teach 1 to free himself from a denial
defender.
3. To teach 3 the proper techniques of face-guard pressure,
denial, and sagging.
4. To teach 3 how to delay the two-on-one fast break until
defensive help arrives, and to teach 1 and 2 how to attack
a lone defender.
5. All of our full court drills are multi-purpose, teaching
many of the offensive and defensive phases of our full
court game.

The Three Drill Defensively

Procedure (Diagram 3-16):
1. Line players up as in the three drill offensively. It is easy
for the players to remember the drills: three drill—three
men; offensively (two attackers, one defender), defensively (two defenders, one attacker).
2. 1, 2, and 3 perform the same duties on their trip
downcourt as they did in the three drill offensively.
3. After 2 gets the rebound, however, he does not throw
the ball to 1 because 1 has become a defender. Instead, 2
tries to dribble the length of the court against the repeated double-teams of 1 and 3.
4. 1 and 3 try to force 2 to dribble off the court, exiting by
the baseline corner.

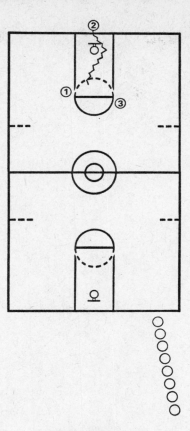

Diagram 3-16

Objectives:

1. To condition players for the full court defensive game.
2. To teach 1 the fine art of driving for a lay-up, and to teach 2 to catch 1 before the lay-up.
3. To teach 1 and 3 proper double-teaming techniques, and to teach the two defenders how to control and dominate one attacker.
4. To teach two defenders how to stop the one-on-two fast break.

The Four Drill Defensively

Procedure (Diagram 3-17):

1. Line players up at the end line as in the other drills.

2. 1, 2, and 3 have the same responsibilities on their trip downcourt as in the other drills.
3. 4 either short-stops on 1 or puts out-of-bounds pressure on 2. If 4 plays 2, then he must keep 2 from spotting 1 or from passing cleanly to him.
4. Once the ball is in-bounded, 3 and 4 defend against 1 and 2. 3 and 4 can run any of the two-man stunts mentioned in Chapter 2.
5. 3 and 4 fast-break if they steal the ball.

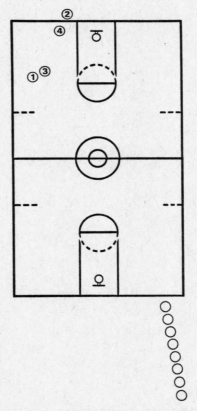

Diagram 3-17

Objectives:
1. To condition players for full court pressure defense.
2. To perfect face-guarding and denial techniques.

3. To teach short-stopping.
4. To teach 3 and 4 full court man-to-man pressure defense, double-teaming, run and jumps, traps, switches and other defensive tactics.
5. To teach proper methods of pressuring the in-bounds passer.

The Five Drill Defensively

Procedure (Diagram 3-18):

1. Line all players up at the end of the court as in the other drills.
2. 1, 2, and 3 perform the same maneuvers on the trip downcourt as in the other drills. 4 takes 2, the out-of-bounds passer. 5, however, can short-stop, center-field,

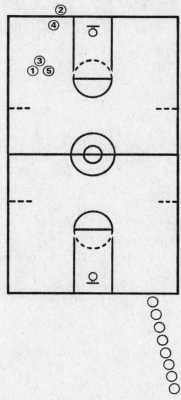

Diagram 3-18

double on the out-of-bounds passer, or left-field. The coach can let 5 decide or he can dictate the coverage he wants.
3. When the ball is passed in-bounds, 3, 4, and 5 run repeated three-man run and jumps, traps, switches or any defensive stunt the coach wants them to work on. 1 and 2 attempt to break the pressure.
4. If 3, 4, and 5 intercept, and interceptions should be the rule rather than the exception, they fast-break against 1 and 2.

Objectives:

1. To condition players for full court pressure defense.
2. To teach 4 proper techniques for guarding the passer.
3. To teach short-stopping center-fielding, left-fielding, and so on.
4. To teach our three-man defensive stunts.
5. To teach trapping techniques and fast-breaking off steals.

The Six Drill Defensively

Procedure (Diagram 3-19):

1. Line the squad up at the end of the court as in the three, four, and five drills.
2. 1, 2, 3, and 4 perform the same maneuvers downcourt as they did in the other drills. 6, however, races downcourt to the end line and then comes in-bounds to receive a pass from 2. 5 defends against 6.
3. 4 can drop off 2 and short-stop or center-field.
4. If ball is in-bounded, 3, 4, and 5 use any of our defensive stunts for the length of the court. Any interception should be followed by a fast break, and the same six begin the drill again.

Objectives:

1. To condition players for the full court pressure defense.
2. To teach 3, 4, and 5 our full court defensive system.
3. To teach the fundamentals presented in this chapter.

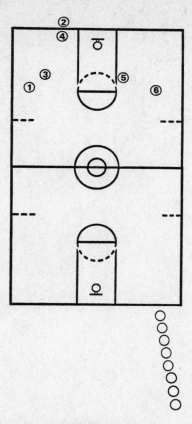

Diagram 3-19

4

Strategies for Stopping Advancement of the Ball

Zone press coaches can use the techniques and drills presented in the first three chapters to improve their favorite zone press. Coaches whose teams have little time to prepare for their opening game can teach those techniques and drills not only as a foundation for their future man-to-man team presses, but also as an adequate full court pressure defense for the early-season games. Coaches who want to continue their development of the full court man-to-man pressure defenses will read and teach the material in this chapter; and all coaches who may someday face a good man-to-man full court pressure defense will need to read and understand this chapter.

FORCE CHANGE OF DIRECTION

Unless a certain direction has been called ("fan" or "funnel"), the individual defender on the ball must force the dribbler to change his direction (zig-zag drill) as often as possible. However, the teammates of the dribbler's defender can stop another change of direction with the word "help." When the defender on the dribbler hears "help," he knows that one of his teammates plans a stunt if he can continue channelling the dribbler toward that helper. After the helper (trapper) picks up the dribbler, the container leaves to take his new man. Good dribblers have learned to loop out of defensive switching stunts by keeping their dribble alive. The dribbler's new defender (the original trapper) now begins forcing more changes of direction until he hears "help." When he hears "help," he channels the dribbler toward it.

Defensive teams can force changes of direction all the way downfloor, hoping for an individual dribbling mistake. Or, they can force changes of direction until they hear "help." Or, defenders can fan or funnel (see later section in this chapter). Or, they can force changes of direction until they hear the first "help"; and after that first defensive assignment change the defense can fan or funnel. Or, they can fan or funnel; and after the first defensive stunt the defense can spontaneously react to "help." These last two strategies can cause chaos for any offensive team that has not drilled against them.

GIVE THE OUTSIDE, THEN TAKE IT AWAY

Individual defenders can give the outside, instead of forcing the dribbler to constantly change his direction. When the defender does give the outside, he usually has a pre-arranged moment to take it away. His teammates are aware of the moment of change, and the defender directly parallel to the dribbler comes hard offering help. A trapping or a switching stunt occurs. This can be followed by a fan or a funnel. Such strategies give defenders a spontaneous reaction to offensive movement, followed by a defensive arrangement equal to zone presses.

Two spontaneous defensive maneuvers can follow or be followed by a called one. Traps or jumps can be spontaneous or pre-called. Traps prevent the looping dribblers from advancing the ball, forcing them to pick up their dribble.

STEALING THE PASS

Good gap shooters leave their men at the exact moment that the trapper leaves his. When gap shooters are that alert, they usually arrive as the obvious pass is being thrown. A steal often results.

But basketball players' reactions and alertness are not always ideal. However, when the gap shooter does commit, he cannot hesitate. He must race hard to his new assignment. While racing toward that new attacker, the gap shooter decides to steal the pass, deny the pass, delay the attack, or draw the charge.

If the pass has not been thrown, the gap shooter has the option of staying one step off the line between the ball and the receiver or moving into the lane between the ball and the receiver. He can use variety, alternating between the two. If one option has been more successful, he may wish to continue the momentum. If the defense has a chance for a ten-second violation, if the passer is inexperienced or somewhat conservative, or if the receiver does not move well without the ball, the denial defense would reap a better harvest. But if we need the basketball, then one step off the line between the receiver and the ball could result in an interception.

If the pass has been thrown and there is no chance for an interception, the gap shooter must decide between drawing the charge or delaying the next offensive move. Should the new receiver be racing to receive a lead pass and the gap shooter have an opportunity to get set before contact, we prefer to draw the charge. But if these two conditions do not exist, we want the gap shooter to arrive as the ball arrives, bellying up against the new receiver. Sometimes this receiver will walk, sometimes he will pass to another teammate, sometimes he will fake and begin a dribble; but almost always he delays momentarily before he considers any option because of the unexpected instant defensive pressure.

When the gap shooter does not get to the receiver in time, he must approach the potential dribbler with a fence slide. He should never play the dribbler head up. He should move to the attacker's inside shoulder, using his arms to deflect any pass to the middle, forcing the attacker to take the longer route to the basket by dribbling outside. The defender should gradually close and put more pressure on the dribbler. He should stay a half-step ahead. He should keep his inside hand (trail hand) down to steal any crossover dribble. He could then take the outside away, activating the giving-the-outside-then-taking-it-away stunt. A teammate located inside would be coming to trap or jump.

FAN

When all defenders know the direction the defender on the ball intends to channel the dribbler, the gap shooters can cheat an extra step toward intended receivers. This cheating can make the difference in an interception.

"Fan" is the word used for ball defenders to direct the dribbler down the outside lanes of the court (Diagram 4-1). It can be called from the bench or from the floor.

When a defender has the initial ball handler, he has no way of knowing where his teammates are. He has his back to all downcourt defenders. To cut a dribbler in the direction where there is no defending teammate would free the dribbler to drive into front court. So the nearest teammate to the defender on the ball can call "help" if he is located in the outside driving lanes, or "fan" even if he is stationed in an inside lane (see Diagram 4-3).

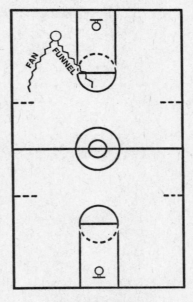

Diagram 4-1

Upon hearing "fan," the dribbler's defender cuts his man toward the outside.

Diagram 4-2 depicts a fan technique. X1 fans 1 toward X4. X4 can call "jump" or "trap." X3, who has cheated toward 4, eliminates that passing lane. X2 closes the passing lane to 3. X1's body shields the pass to 2. When 1 picks up his dribble or when X1 hears "jump," he runs his fish hook route to cover 2. Adequate pressure will force the turnover.

A defender need not occupy space in an outside lane to run a fan stunt effectively. For example, there is no defender in the outside lane in Diagram 4-3, but X2 knows "fan" has been called. X1 must fan the dribbler outside. X2 races over to stop 1's dribble advancement. X3 cheats toward 2 because he is aware that "fan" has been called. X5 fudges to the passing lane between 1 and 3. X4 can cover both 4 and 5 should X2 command X1 to trap. If X2 yells "jump," X1 would fish hook until he found 4, the open man.

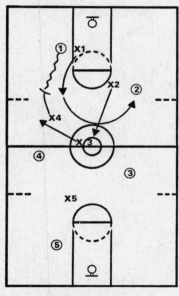

Diagram 4-2

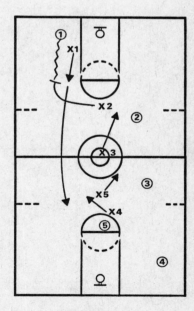

Diagram 4-3

FUNNEL

If, however, the initial dribbler's defender hears "funnel," he cuts his man to the inside lane. As long as the dribbler stays in the middle lane, we will run and jump but not trap. But if he ventures into the far outside lane, we would either trap or jump, whichever the trapper wishes to call.

When all the other teammates of the dribbler's defender hear "funnel," they can cheat a step or so in the direction of the ball and gamble for a steal. It gives the gap shooters an added step in the direction of the obvious pass.

It is most difficult for a dribbler to drive in one direction and pass across his body in the opposite direction without having the fanner or funneler deflect the ball. The dribbler might pick up his dribble and pivot to pass in the opposite direction. But the container should have released and be denying a pass to this new pass receiver (see Diagram 4-4).

Let's say X1 funnels 1 toward X2. X2 runs and jumps. X3, knowing that "funnel" has been called, covers the obvious pass-

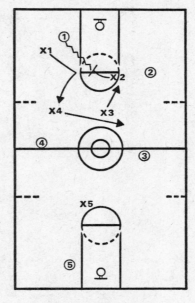

Diagram 4-4

ing lane to 2. X4, also knowing "funnel" has been called and knowing that X1 will deflect a pass to 4, leaves early and shoots the gap on 3. X1 rotates to 4. If 1 picks up his dribble, and if X2's teammates deny all passes, a turnover will result.

FAN OR FUNNEL (LET THE OFFENSE CALL IT)

After a few fans or funnels, the opposition figures "fan" means outside while "funnel" means inside. This leaves us with three options: taking a time-out each time we wish to change, reverse the meanings orally, or let the offense call it. We only have five time-outs so this method could only be used five times. Occasionally, we reverse the meanings. When we change from the bench we call "fan invert" to mean funnel and "funnel invert" to mean fan. Sometimes we even go further. We reverse the meanings in a time-out huddle. When we do that, "fan" would mean funnel and "funnel" would be fan, and "fan invert" would be fan and "funnel invert" would be funnel. This can keep the opposition guessing. And, of course, these meanings can be changed from game to game, from quarter to quarter, from time-out to time-out.

Mostly, we let the offense call it. This merely eliminates our gap shooters from cheating a step or so. And we can still call "fan" or "funnel" from the bench during time-outs.

An example of a good plan for the fourth quarter: fan the first two minutes, funnel the next three, and fan the last three. Under this strategy nothing needs to be called verbally. Players need only be aware of the time remaining.

You can fan on even score or even time (minutes left) and funnel on odd score or odd time, or vice versa. There are many ways to pre-arrange the fan or funnel signals, thereby eliminating any need to call them from the bench.

However, there are times when you need to call them from the bench. For example, you pre-planned as in the fourth-quarter example above. But fan is causing chaotic conditions in the opposition's attack. So you adjust by yelling "fan." This calls off the pre-plan and places your team in fan. When the opposition solves fan, you might want to yell "funnel."

COMING OUT OF DOUBLE-TEAMS

Defensive teams can lose the advantage they gained with a double-team by using bad or sloppy techniques when coming out of an unsuccessful trap. The container, of course, must rotate to the new open attacker while the trapper remains with the double-teamed player.

There are only two ways a double-team can be broken: by a dribble or by a pass. Although a dribbler should never successfully escape good double-teamers, it occasionally happens. When the dribbler does clear the double-teamers, the trapper (assuming he has yelled "trap" and he has been driven around) must cut the dribbler toward the nearest sideline, trying to bring him under control. Meanwhile, the container should have covered the open attacker (see last section in this chapter). Any defender on the side of the court of the dribbler can initiate another run and jump or trap or hedging maneuver to help the trapper control the free dribbler.

If the opposition passes out of double-teams, then the two double-teamers must not watch the flight of the pass. The container must race hard to find the open attacker. Often, his man is the pass receiver. His man will be further downcourt if another defender shot the gap on the pass receiver. Although this defender should not watch the flight of the ball, he should be aware of the position of both his man and the ball.

The trapper must cover his man after the completed pass. Too often this player middle-cuts to receive a return pass which will break the press. The trapper's first step should be in the direction of the pass. He should open slightly to the ball, and he must begin a quick slide (or stride if it is a long pass) to get his body above the advancement of the ball.

Upon passing the ball, the trapped attacker has only four options immediately available: the backdoor, the give-and-go, the diagonal, and remain to receive a return pass. The defensive technique of stepping toward the new pass receiver and sliding with an open stance toward him eliminates the give-and-go and the diagonal cuts by the original passer, forcing both moves to be considered a backdoor cut. In order for the new pass receiver to successfully complete the backdoor cut, he must either lob the pass or bounce-pass through two defenders (the man guarding the passer and the man guarding the receiver). The bounce pass is slow and should be stolen. The lob pass could be picked off by another weakside defender, or it could be deflected by the backdoor cutter's defender. Also, backdoor cutters are more susceptible to charging (see Chapter 1).

The trapped attacker's other option of remaining to receive a return pass is not an attacking move. A return pass constitutes a vertical pass away from the attacking end of the court. We would not try to intercept such a pass. We would permit its completion and then begin our stunts again. But the offense would have far less than ten seconds to get the ball into front court.

TRAPS AND SWITCHING

Almost all players will keep their dribble alive, looping out of any run and jump or switching maneuver. Seldom, if ever, will the poised dribbler pick up his dribble. So, the defense should trap all players who aspire to keep their dribble alive.

Players who will pick up their dribble should be defended by a run and jump or another switching tactic. If an attacker passes quickly off the dribble, many times to the obvious pass receiver, the defense should run and jump. A defensive gap shooter would steal the pass.

RUN AND JUMPS

Run and jumps work best against inexperienced, unpoised dribblers. Dribblers who have not been taught to keep their dribble alive, who pass off the dribble, and who throw the obvious pass can be forced into errors with the run and jump.

Defensive teams that run and jump for a few possessions prior to activating the area man-to-man press lead attacking teams into an ambush. Where the run and jumps have weaknesses, the area man-to-man has strengths. Yet, they look so similar (see Chapter 8).

BEST AREAS TO DOUBLE-TEAM

All players must be taught and constantly made aware of the best areas to double-team. Gap shooters as well as trappers need this information. It must always be uppermost in each defender's mind. Only then can the five defenders respond as one; only then can they achieve the highest degree of defensive efficiency.

Chalk talks and handouts present the most effective means of communicating the best double-team areas to the players. Constant drilling, correcting mistakes as they occur, solidifies that knowledge.

A ROTATION DRILL TO STOP
AN ESCAPED DRIBBLER'S ADVANCEMENT

Our basic rule, a weakside defender stops the free dribbler, corresponds with our coverage from the double-team. If 1 dribbles baseline on X1, X1 stays with him (Diagram 4-5). If 1 drives sideline on X2, X2 covers 1. If 1 splits X1 and X2 with a dribble, 1 becomes the responsibility of the defender who has his back to the defensive basket (Diagram 4-5). We cannot permit confusion to exist between X1, X2, and X3. If we are to play the best defense possible during each possession, they must each know their duties. In Diagram 4-5, X1 would have X2's man if X2 had originally been the trapper. If X1 was the trapper, then he would take back the man that he left when he ordered the trap. X2, the defender with his back to the defensive basket, guards 1, the escaped dribbler. X3 and X2 would switch men if X3 called "jump."

Procedure (Diagram 4-5):
1. Line players up at end court. Rotate from 1 to X1 to X2 to X3 to end of line.
2. 1 can split X1 and X2 or 1 can drive outside X1 or outside X2. X3 plays as a weakside defender, regardless of the direction 1 chooses to drive.
3. The coach activates the drill by passing in-bounds to 1. X1 and X2 apply the double-team. 1 tries to dribble around X1 and X2. X1 and X2 try to push 1 out of the corner.

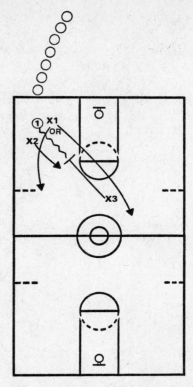

Diagram 4-5

4. Should 1 escape the double-team, X3 stops the dribbler, yelling "trap." X2 and X1 must recognize who is to stay and trap and who has downcourt responsibilities. X2, in the diagram, has trapping duties.

5. Sometimes we designate X2 as the trapper. In this case, when 1 splits X2 and X1 with a dribble, X1 would cut behind X2 and the dribbler in order to achieve downcourt position on the man X2 just left.

6. At first, 1 picks up his dribble momentarily, allowing X1 time to get further downcourt. Later, we let 1 loop out of the double-team of X2 and X3 while X1 stations himself as the weakside defender. X1 becomes the new weakside defender, assuming responsibility for stopping the escaped dribbler. X3 and X2 trap while 1 tries to escape and the drill continues downcourt and back.

Objectives:

1. To teach trapping.
2. To teach the looping dribble technique.
3. To teach weakside to stop the escaped dribbler.
4. To teach defensive trappers to recognize who covers the dribbler once the double-team has been broken. This eliminates the confusion that sometimes results in an unplanned, futile triple-team.

5

Principles of
the Man-to-Man
Full Court Press

Clearly worded, easily defined principles, when presented by the coach to his players, can bring team cohesiveness to what otherwise might appear to be random drilling. The defensive coach must never permit any player to violate any of these ten cardinal concepts. Any violation must be corrected immediately. Coaches must explain all exceptions thoroughly.

Each principle outlined in this chapter blends perfectly with all our stunts. And, these tenets lead directly to our area man-to-man press (see Chapter 8).

DENY ALL PENETRATION TO THE MIDDLE LANE

When the ball penetrates into the middle lane, it has eight primary escape routes, five of which are downcourt (attacking) passing lanes. However, the defense at best has only four defenders off the ball. Mathematics tells us that we cannot adequately cover five passing lanes with a maximum of four defenders. Reason compels us to conclude that penetration of the ball into the middle lane will break any press, especially one that double-teams the ball.

When the ball has entered the middle lane, by dribble or by pass, it is best for the other defenders to cover the downcourt lanes from the inside out. A direct pass down the middle lane would result in an easy score. Forcing the pass to the sideline would not only dampen an immediate score, but it could allow the defense time to recover and regroup to press again.

Scoring damage frequently occurs when the offense gets the ball to the middle lane; but there are times when the defense will direct the ball there. Sometimes we run two- and three-man stunts into the middle lane. Sometimes we use a team technique, such as funneling, to influence the offense to go where we want. These exceptions must be made clear to the defenders, and the reasons why should be understood (see stunting areas of this book).

DENY ALL VERTICAL PASSES

A succession of completed downcourt passes will defeat full court pressuring defenses. While we know it is impossible to deny all vertical passes, we want it to be the goal of our pressuring man-to-man defense. Frequently, by denying or appearing to deny downcourt passes, defenders encourage potential passers to become dribblers. This activates many of our stunts. And if this ball handler passes quickly off his dribble, we have a better chance to steal the pass than if the passer were standing, pivoting, and looking for an open pass receiver. Our defense wants to impel the dribble, and then we want to stop it, stealing any pass off of it.

DOUBLE-TEAM ALL PLAYER AND BALL CROSSINGS

Some dribblers like to use screeners to help free themselves for an uncontested dribble into front court. Some cutters inadvertently cut near a dribbler, trying to receive a pass on a middle cut. By double-teaming these prototypes, we force the dribbler to pick up the ball. Often, the dribbler will make the obvious pass to the screener as he rolls or to the middle cutter as he progresses downcourt. These attackers are moving away from the passer, making the pass easier to intercept. A nearby defending teammate of the double-teamers could shoot the gap for an interception. Another defender, further downcourt, could draw the charge on the cutter or compel the walking violation upon reception of the obvious pass.

More importantly, however, offensive-minded teams will begin to avoid the congregation of the ball and two attackers. This leaves the dribbler in a clearout situation, giving defensive teammates of the dribbler's defender more time to achieve better defensive coverage. It also invites a longer passing attack, and longer passes are easier to intercept.

Teams that run and jump switch or trap exclusively do not need this principle, for no two offensive players could screen and roll or otherwise congregate near the ball. For example, an attacker who wishes to screen on the ball could never reach the ball handler. His defender, who is closer to the passer when playing denial defense, would be jumping before the screener arrived.

FLOAT ON PLAYERS MORE THAN ONE PASS AWAY

The offensive player nearest the ball in all downcourt passing lanes must be denied the pass. A completed pass would advance the ball and defeat the press. But a second receiver in any passing lane or one located more than 20 feet away from the ball could not receive a direct pass if his defender floated properly. Floaters are in a position to wreck most press attacks. Floaters can run and jump a dribbler; they have a few advance steps in shooting gaps between passers and potential receivers; they can deflect or intercept chest or bounce passes to their assigned man; they can deflect any lob pass to their assigned man; they can stop a loose dribbler; and they can draw charges from any downcourt cutter.

Floaters play their men physically, but they operate in the passing lanes mentally. They always locate one step off the line between their men and the ball for every 20 feet they are away from the ball. They also situate two-thirds the distance from the ball and one-third the distance from their man.

KEEP PROPER SPACING

Every defender must maintain proper spacing if the team defense is to obtain maximum results. The defender on the ball must stay one arm-length away from the dribbler, pushing him

toward the called defensive stunt. Defenders on the first attackers in each passing lane must deny passes to their appointed
men, forcing the ball handler to dribble or throw a lob pass.
Floaters must be properly spaced, ready to initiate one of their
many options once the defensive team stunt springs into motion.

Each defender must readjust his position every time the
ball travels, the attacker with the ball moves, or his assigned
man roams. The need for adjustment, no matter how slight,
must be recognized instantly; and the proper corrections made
simultaneously. One step, one pass, or one dribble requires a
new position, a new spacing. Defensive coaches must insist
upon it.

When the offense skips a man in a normal passing route
(Diagram 5-1), that pass can easily be intercepted. The defense
can encourage the offense to skip a man by playing the next pass
receiver tight and appearing to play the second pass receiver
away loose. This loose defender, however, anticipates the pass,
goes for and gains the interception.

EVERY DEFENDER MUST BE AHEAD OF THE BALL

Horizontal passes and those thrown away from the offensive
basket are not contested. They are not attacking maneuvers, so
their completion does not hurt the team defense.

Attacking vertical passes harm the team defense. And although these passes are denied, they are sometimes successful.
When the opposition completes a downcourt pass, all defenders
must recover while the ball is in the air to a defensive position
beyond the advancement of the ball. Players who consistently
arrive tardy will not make good pressers. The players should be
told this, keeping them aware of their responsibilities and this
principle.

Dribblers sometimes escape the maze of defenders who try
to prevent the dribbling penetration. When this happens, the
deepest weakside defender stops the dribbler (see another section in this chapter) while all other defenders race to get above
the ball. The weakside defender, located directly above the
deepest weakside defender, must race hard to stop the obvious
pass to the area just vacated by the deepest defender.

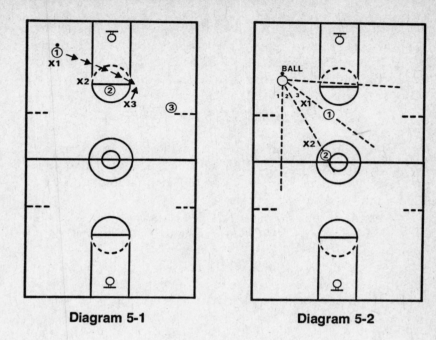

| Diagram 5-1 | Diagram 5-2 |

When all defenders reachieve proper positioning above the ball, another stunt can be called, another interception attempted. This principle keeps all defenders aware of the location of the ball and their man. It helps to prevent the lay-up. It results in many hustling steals.

PHYSICALLY FLOAT—MENTALLY PLAY PASSING LANE

All floaters must know where their men are, where the ball is, and where all the nearby passing lanes are. Each floater must play his own man and mentally cover the other nearby passing lanes (Diagram 5-2). X2, a floater in Diagram 5-2, would cover passing lanes 1, 2, and 3. X2 would also try to draw the charge on any lob pass to 1 or any other cutter in his immediate area. Should the ball handler dribble toward X1, X1 might choose to activate a stunt, such as a run and jump. X2 must decide immediately whether to become a gap shooter on the man X1 just left or to hold his position.

Of all defenders, floaters have the best opportunity to force turnovers. They must remain alert to every movement of the ball and men. They must read well and be daring. To a great extent, their play determines the success or failure of the press.

WEAKSIDE DEFENDER STOPS DRIBBLER

A loose dribbler, unless stopped, will penetrate to the goal for an uncontested lay-up. We want to force at least one more pass, which might be stolen, deflected, or mishandled, before yielding the uncontested lay-up.

Because he has sagged and should easily see the dribbler breaking free, we want the deepest defender on the weakside to stop the escaped dribbler. We like to impel the dribble penetration because dribbling moves the ball slower downfloor than passing. The dribbler will sometimes break free, making this an extremely important principle.

When the deepest weakside defender approaches the loose dribbler, the dribbler will frequently make the obvious (and penetrating) pass to the man the deepest weakside defender just left. Unless a teammate has been drilled on a proper rotation, a lay-up will still result. Letting the deepest weakside defender stop the dribble penetration also conforms to our half-court defensive rules, permitting us to teach only one set of rules and thus making matters simpler for our players.

Stopping the Dribbler Drill

Procedure (Diagram 5-3):

1. We only use four players; the others can be managers. Rotate from 1 to X2 to 4 to X4 to end of the line.
2. This drill is also good for preventing the fast-break lay-up. Often, we can gain a steal by forcing one more pass.
3. X4 makes himself as big as possible as he approaches the dribbler, 1. X4 pushes 1 toward the outside. X4 tries to deflect any pass made to 4 too early. When X4 sees that X2 can intercept a bounce pass to 4, X4 immediately pressures 1 with his hands waving from his waist and over his head. This encourages the slow bounce pass. X2 knows that X4 will initially induce the bounce pass, and

he prepares himself for it. After X2 has had time to recover, X4 will want to keep his hands in the same plane as the ball. X4 might deflect the ball as it comes out of the passer's hand.

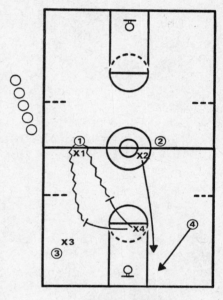

Diagram 5-3

4. Many times, X4 can hedge toward the breakaway dribbler, slowing him down, allowing the dribbler's defender to recover, and stop the dribbler himself.
5. When 4 sees X4 go to pick up 1, he breaks to the goal.
6. When X2 sees 1 driving by X1, he sprints downfloor to cover 4. If there had been a defender, X3, and the coach can activate 3 and X3, he could sink toward the goal and help. However, the weakside, X4 and X2, are always responsible for the proper rotation. X1 would rotate around and pick up 2 should the defense successfully halt the dribbling penetration.

Objectives:

1. To teach X4 to stop the breakaway dribbler.
2. To teach X2 to race downfloor for deep defense, replacing X4. We frequently steal this pass.

3. To teach proper defensive rotation in a case of a defensive breakdown.

RELOCATE AS BALL IS PASSED

When the ball, the man with the ball, or a defender's assigned man moves, the defender must adjust his positioning. Passing offers the quickest method to advance the ball. So when the ball is passed, every defender must adjust quickly. We want this adjustment to occur while the pass is in the air, not after the ball has reached the intended receiver.

All defenders must move to reachieve proper coverage and proper spacing. The best way to drill for this is to place four non-moveable attackers at strategic spots on the court with a defender on each of them. The defenders are instructed not to deflect or steal the passes, but they are to run to their proper new positions when each pass is thrown. They must reach these positions by the time the receivers catch the ball. The coach should blow his whistle as the receiver catches the ball. All defenders must stop when they hear the whistle. The coach can recognize which defenders are in proper position and which are not. The coach can position the attackers at different spots on different days, drilling on different situations. The passer should be permitted to fake a pass in one direction, then pass in another.

NEVER GIVE THE LAY-UP

A lay-up costs two points. It is rarely missed in modern-day basketball.

If we can force the attacker off-balance, we will allow him to shoot his lay-up. If, however, it is a clear driving lay-up, we want to draw the charge or prevent the bunny. If we have time to position ourselves for the charge, we trade the two points for the offensive foul. We hope that someday the rules committee will adopt the National Basketball Association's rule of not allowing a basket that is scored during the commitment of an offensive foul. If we cannot achieve position to draw the charge, we want our defender to hit both arms of the driver-shooter very hard, not permitting the three-point play and trying to steal the ball on the way up. In order to get his two points, the driver-shooter still has to make two shots from 15 feet away. The only time we call this rule off is when we have a lead late in a game and we do not want the clock stopped.

TRANSITION: A PRESS DRILL
WHEN YOU DON'T SCORE

Transition has become a most talked about subject by basketball coaches. Coaches simply do not wish to give the easy basket while converting from offense to defense. They want the offensive basket on such conversions. Defensive coaches must work out an orderly method of retreat after they lose possession of the ball. If that method of retreat also includes a double-teaming man-to-man pressure defense, then the defense can pressure whether it scores or not.

This transition drill is used after a missed free throw or an unsuccessful field goal. A full court zone or man-to-man press is difficult to organize unless the offensive team scores. So when a team has a poor shooting night and is behind, the transition drill will prove to be a definite advantage.

If we score, we immediately go into our press or one of our stunts. If we do not score and do not activate the transition drill, we retreat in a straight line with a sprint to half-court before turning and racing backward, picking up our assigned attacker.

Most teams, regardless of their patterns or style of play, send three and one-half men to the offensive boards and leave one and one-half back for defense. The transition drill begins from this positioning (Diagram 5-4).

X2 is in a good position to challenge the defense for the long rebound; X2 is in a good position to receive a tip-out from X4, X5, or X3 should they be unable to establish a good offensive rebounding position; and X2 is in an excellent position to pressure the guard who has the responsibility of receiving the outlet pass on a fast-break ball club. X1 is answerable for deep defense. X3, X4, and X5 are accountable for rebounding and, if success-

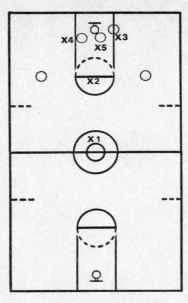

Diagram 5-4

ful, putting the rebound back in for two and often three points. If X3, X4, and X5 cannot get the offensive rebound, they apply the initial double-team of the transition drill.

For maximum effectiveness, the two guards must know the duties of both X1 and X2 as they will frequently have to interchange positions. All three frontliners must also know the obligations of X3, X4, and X5 because different offensive patterns place them in different offensive rebounding positions.

Diagrams 5-5 and 5-6 display a rebound secured by our opponents on the left and on the right side of the floor. X2 is the interceptor of any quickly thrown outlet pass to the sidelines. The off-side rebounder covers the outlet pass at the free throw line.

During the game or previously by scouting, the coach should have detected the favorite avenue for the opposition's outlet pass. Many teams like to designate a particular ball handler to run their break. X2 can face-guard this ball handler, eliminating immediately the opposition's quick break.

When the drill is activated during a game, X2 can cover this designated dribbler or he can take the outlet pass area on the side of the rebound (as shown in Diagrams 5-5 and 5-6). Adjustments may have to be made depending on the length of time one intends to use the drill as a press. X5 is the double-teaming defender, regardless of the side from which the opposition secures the rebound. X4 and X3 have the same reponsibilities but on different sides of the court.

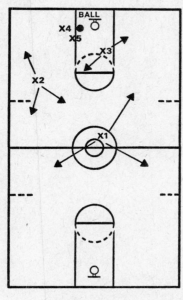 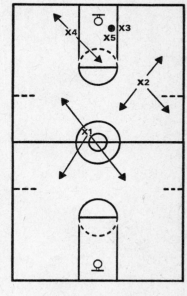

Diagram 5-5   **Diagram 5-6**

The defender who is double-teaming with X5 must not let the rebounder take a dribble between himself and X5. The defense should encourage the rebounder to dribble into the corner. He is usually a tall man who is among the team's poorest dribblers and ball handlers. Once the rebounder reaches the corner, it is easier to apply the double-team as well as cover the downcourt passing lanes (Diagrams 5-7 and 5-8). Also, the man with the ball will have lost one of his advantages—the dribble.

The defensive rebounder opposite the double-team must be sure that the ball is not thrown immediately to his side of the court—his stealing a pass from this position assures him a lay-up.

As the new offensive team moves downcourt, X3 or X4 must be sure that the opposition's guard has not moved to the opposite corner from the rebound for an easy outlet pass and a drive down the sideline. If we are not man-to-man pressing, we permit this pass which stops the quick break and we retreat to our downfloor defense.

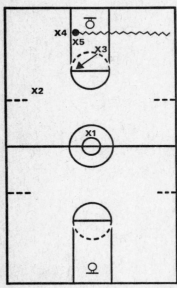

Diagram 5-7

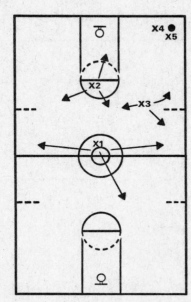

Diagram 5-8

X3 or X4 is also charged with covering the outlet pass down the center of the court if the offensive guard has moved into the corner on the side of the rebound. X3 and X4 must check this possibility first. It is the more dangerous to transition defense. X1 is in charge of the deep defense and the interception of any long lob pass.

The drill is not over should the rebounder pass the ball into the corner, unless we are only concerned with transition defense. The new offensive team can still be trapped, but they will probably have a better ball handler with the ball.

Assume that the ball has been passed out to the left corner (Diagram 5-9), the same side as the rebound. X2 must prevent

an immediate drive by the offense, containing him until X4 can
get there for the double-team. X5 drops back to the center of the
free throw line for the interception of a pass thrown there. X3 or
X1 covers the passing lane on the left sideline while X3 or X1
covers deep for a long pass or a lob pass. There is a rule that
governs whether X3 or X1 covers deep: If X3 had to guard a pass
to the corner opposite the rebound, because an offensive guard
was there, then X3 must cover deep; but if there were no attacker in his corner, he could easily move into the center, then
into the sideline passing lane.

Suppose the pass is made to the corner across the court
from the area where the rebound was secured (Diagram 5-10).
X3 would have been covering the guard in the corner according
to our first rule. If X3 is unable to intercept this pass, he must
contain the new ball handler until X5 can arrive for the double-
team. X4, who had been double-teaming the rebounder, releases to the center of the free throw line to cover the passing
lane there. X2 covers deep while X1 takes the side passing lane.

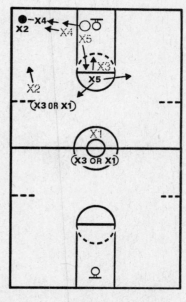

Diagram 5-9

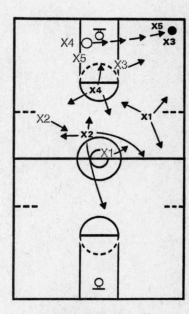

Diagram 5-10

We consider the pressing aspects of this drill another stunt. On nights when we have trouble scoring, we can activate this drill as a stunt and still be able to press. But if we are interested only in transition from offense to defense, we use the initial coverage of Diagrams 5-4, 5-5, and 5-6. Then, we retreat in a straight line to midcourt before relocating our assigned men for pressure defense there.

6

Strategies for
Stunting from the
Full Court Man Press

Often, because of a limited number of pre-season practices, many coaches do not have time to teach an effective team press. These coaches can teach the stunts of this chapter, which they can later blend into our team presses. When time does become available, they can add the stunts of the first four chapters to the principles of Chapters 5 and 6 to get the area man-to-man press.

We begin many games with one of these stunts just to find out our opponent's offensive plans against our team presses. We then activate the team press or stunt which would best counter those offensive plans (see Chapters 7 and 8). These stunts also provide a change of pace, a surprise move that might cause a turnover, from our basic man-to-man press.

THREE-MEN-AND-A-TANDEM

Three defenders offering pressure while two play safe defines the three-men-and-a-tandem press. The three men can offer extreme pressure because they know the two safeties can cover any mistake, any freed attacker. These three defenders can face-guard the first two attackers downfloor and pressure the out-of-bounds passer, or they can face-guard the first two attackers downfloor while the defender on the out-of-bounds passer can play short stop or left field (see Chapter 3). Or, they can also face-guard the first three receivers downfloor, eliminating coverage on the out-of-bounds passer.

Once the ball is in-bounded, these three defenders can run and jump trap or switch, blitz trap or switch, give the outside and then take it away, or use any trap or switch described in Chapters 2 or 4. Any steals or turnovers will add to the victory margin, but this stunt does not have to cause turnovers to be effective. It can speed up a team, or the coach can use it to slow a team down. It can be used just to keep pressure on the offense. It is a drill which we activate during a game, usually at the very beginning. It is something for which most offenses are unprepared. It is a safe stunt, rarely conceding an easy jump shot or a lay-up.

Tandem men play according to their ability. If they are big and quick, we bring the quicker ones down to midcourt and station the slower ones at the defensive free throw line. This gives the impression of a 1-2-1-1 full court zone press. Often, the opposition will show how they intend to attack a team press when they see this defensive line-up. We have one assistant coach who immediately diagrams their attack. We study this diagram to determine which of our team presses would be the most effective. At some point during the game we employ that press.

These tandem defenders can drop completely to the defensive free throw line and defend in a tandem. Or, they can play two defenders who have gone deep man-to-man if the offense chooses to attack with only three men. But if the offense attacks with two men (giving us three-on-two on their defensive end), the tandem defenders locate in the gaps between the three downcourt attackers, deflecting or intercepting any long pass thrown toward either of the three (Diagram 6-1). Three attackers cannot spread themselves in the limited area of the front court where we cannot gap them. In Chapter 7, we will show our three-on-two and our three-on-three downcourt drills.

We teach these tandem defenders a stunt which the deep three defenders know and can make use of. The tandem defender on the foul circle shades the dribbling attacker to one side, channelling the dribbler in one direction. The deeper tandem defender stations himself in full view of the dribbler, a step or two in the direction the dribbler has been channelled. This not only slows the dribbler, allowing the first tandem defender to defend him, but it makes the dribbler aware that the open lane is in the opposite direction. This slows down the offensive attack, giving one of the three deep pressure defenders time to recover and close that lane.

We use a two-on-two drill to teach the three downcourt defenders that they will always have time to recover.

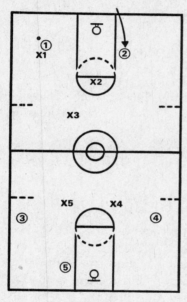

Diagram 6-1   **Diagram 6-2**

Procedure (Diagram 6-2):

1. Line players up as shown. Rotate from X1 to 1 to X5 to 2 to end of the line.
2. 1 and 2 begin at the 28-foot mark. 2 initiates the drill with a dribble which tells 1, 2, and X1 to begin moving toward the basket.
3. X1 starts behind midcourt. He takes the shortest route toward the defensive goal. 1 and 2 attack X5.
4. When X5 sees that X1 has recovered sufficiently to intercept any pass directed toward 1, X5 challenges 2's

jump shot, spreading himself, cutting 2 baseline, forcing 2 to throw a lob or bounce pass. X1 must intercept this pass. If 2 drives baseline, X1 must draw the charge while X5 attempts to block the shot.

Objectives:

1. To teach X1 to recover and intercept a pass. This shows defenders they are never too late.
2. To teach X5 when to cover the outside jumper.
3. To teach 1 and 2 to attack one defender.

We also use a three-on-three full court drill to teach proper recovery. Three attackers line up on one baseline, intending to fast-break to the other. Three defenders line up at the free throw line (15 feet away), facing the three attackers. The coach tosses the ball to the middle attacker as he calls out one of the defenders' names. The three attackers run a three-lane fast break. The other two defenders race back into a tandem defense to stop the three attackers. The defender whose name was called races to the endline (15 feet away) that the attackers just left—before sprinting the length of the court to help his two teammates defend the fast break. If the two defenders can force one extra pass, the other defender can reach the defensive basket in time to compel a three-on-three game.

Hence, we can press with three men, gaining whatever the attackers will give us; and by hustling back once the front line defense is broken, losing nothing to the offense. The three-men-and-a-tandem is a safe stunt, and it will keep the pressure on the attackers (see three-on-two and three-on-three stunts in Chapter 7).

NUMBERING PRESS

Coaches have infinite options for communicating their presses and stunts to their players. They can number areas on the floor and they can number their individual stunts. When they combine the two numbers, they call a stunt in a particular area. For example, 40 could mean full court face-guard pressure and a 7 could represent a blitz trap. 47, therefore, would be a face-guard man-to-man press, followed by a blitz trap when the ball is successfully in-bounded. If they do not combine the two numbers, they would call individual stunts. For example, 40 would indicate a full court face-guard press; and if broken, the defense would retreat into their half-court defense. 7 would mean a blitz trap on an in-bounds pass by the defender on the passer and the receiver. If that is broken, the defense again drops into their half-court defense.

Or, a coach could make it a triple number. In 471, for example, 1 means fan. Now the sequence would be face-guard man-to-man press; followed by a blitz trap on a successful in-bounds pass; and then, if after the next pass the offense still has possession of the ball, the defense cuts the dribbler to the outside for a run and jump stunt.

Such a numbering system can regiment the defense. It can eliminate the thinking and spontaneity that occur when the defense is left free to read situations. We use both: free choice by the defense and control by numbering. Both can win games, and teaching both requires little or no extra time.

We also have a stunt that we call our numbering press stunt. It is simple, easy to teach, and highly effective.

We divide the full court into eight areas (Diagram 6-3). We never double-team in the shaded areas or with two high odd numbers or two high even numbers. In other words, we will not send a man from region 7 to double-team with a man from region 5, nor will we send a man from region 8 to double-team with a man in region 6. The reasoning is quite simple: This would allow our opposition an easy, uncovered shot from the corner within 15 feet. We also do not like two odd men or two even men to double-team, but we do allow this in back court provided that there is no opposite of even or odd near. We do permit two odd or two even men to run and jump switch.

However, by double-teaming with an odd and even man, we have better coverage of the downcourt passing lanes. We can force the obvious pass to be a cross-court pass. If we can compel the bounce or the lob pass, we can possibily intercept.

There are three passing lanes: horizontal, center, and vertical. We cover the lanes with the lowest number on the ball side covering the vertical lane. The next lowest number on the ball side gets the center lane. The lowest number off the ball side gets the horizontal lane. The next lowest number off the ball side gets the center lane. If there is a defensive man in the shaded area, he would get the center lane. In other words, the two smallest numbers get the outside lanes and the largest number on one side gets the center lane. We call this our lane coverage rule.

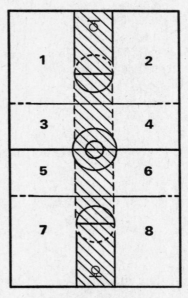

Diagram 6-3

As the reader can observe, the defense begins man-to-man; after the double-team it converts to zone press coverage. A successful pass would have all defenders racing to get above the ball to play the half-court defense.

This stunt commences when the offense does any one of five things: reverses in the back court, isolates a dribbler by sending the other players downfloor, initiates the attack with the first in-bound pass, congests an area as two men and the ball come together, or forces the dribbler to put the ball on the floor. Many great teams, North Carolina for example, will show man and go zone or show zone and go man. This is a stunt that fits such a philosophy.

DROPPING AND DELAYING

This stunt does not steal the ball. It will not cause a turn-over of the ball, only a turnover of the mind. Quick-moving attackers and teams that score a lot of points hate dropping and delaying tactics.

Sometimes, after running some of our other stunts (less than five defenders participating) or one of our team presses (all five men involved), we begin our dropping and delaying strategy. This usually happens about midway the second quarter and lasts deep into the third quarter. Or we will number this press, say 80, and run it off and on between our other stunts. When you run it as 80, you can expect the opposition to throw some long lob passes out-of-bounds.

This press is designed to work on the minds of the dribblers. The ball handler's defender can play his man tight, forcing the dribble, or loose, inviting the dribble. Let's say the in-bounds pass comes to a player in area 1 (Diagram 6-3). The passer cuts opposite the receiver into area 2 and clears out by going into 4, into 6, and finally 8. His defender would stop near the back of area 4. Immediately, the dribbler sums up: A run and jump stunt would occur if I dribble toward area 4. The nearest defender in area 3, 5, or 7 leaves his man and comes to the back of area 3. It appears a run and jump would occur if the dribbler dribbles down the outside lane. He may be tempted to throw a long pass here, especially if he has been trapped or switched several times previously.

However, if he begins to be aggressive with the ball and starts a dribble toward area 4 or area 3, those defenders hedge and drop back, hedge and drop back again. The dribbler begins to wonder when the surprise will occur. But it never comes until we discard 80. When we remove 80 and call another stunt, it is usually very effective. So 80 works on the nerves of the dribbler, helping our overall defensive game plan.

Several teams try to break 80 by flashing an attacker from area 7 or 8 into the middle lane of area 3 or 4. A short pass to this man can lead to another short pass breaking the press. We cover this in two ways: We permit the posting player to receive the pass and drop and delay passes to his teammates; or we have the defenders in area 3 or 4, or both, deny the middle pass, forcing the long lob pass or the dribble penetration. In the former case, it merely means the ball has advanced to area 3 or 4 and someone takes the backside of areas 5 and 6 and we are again dropping and delaying. It also gives the attackers confidence that they can hit the posting player at will; something we can later use to our advantage. When the ball gets into front court, we stop dropping and delaying with everyone defensing the man in their area (usually their assigned man). In both cases, if the defender in area 3 or 4 must pick up the poster (it may be his original assigned man) who broke from area 7 or 8, his teammates must rotate to cover his man. In other words, if the defender in area 3 picks up a man breaking from area 8, then that defender in area 8 must pick up 3's man. Each of these defenders stays with that man until a proper "switch back" can be executed.

BAITING THE DRIBBLER

After dropping and delaying, we may begin to bait the dribbler. Or, we may bait him without ever dropping and delaying, but the two stunts go together like love and marriage. You may give this stunt a number such as 90.

Diagram 6-4 shows our defenders putting the bait on the hook, seeing if the fish will bite. 1 dribbles toward the center lane. X3 hedges a run and jump but retreats. 1 should slow his dribble penetration each time X3 hedges. But X3 does not spring the trap; instead he retreats to cover his man in a denial stance. As 1 crosses midcourt, X1 recovers to 1's left, forcing a reverse or a crossover for 1 to continue penetrating. X2, who has retreated to cover 2, races hard to trap or jump with X1. 2 will break outside to receive a cross-court pass from 1. At first, 1 will be hesitant to make this obvious pass. But if X5 will bait 1 by offering no notice that 1 intends to make this pass, 1's confidence will grow. After three or four possessions, and especially if it is early in the game, 1 will throw the obvious pass without noticing X5's intentions or positioning. That is when X5 will have hooked his fish and should reel him in by shooting the gap and gaining a driving lay-up.

When activated at a strategic moment of the game, this

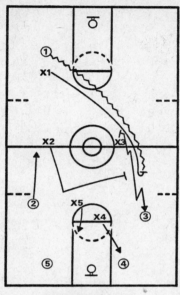

Diagram 6-4

stunt can change the momentum and ultimately the outcome of the contest. An important time: Begin baiting with 2 minutes remaining in the third quarter of a hotly contested game. When the clock winds down to 30 seconds and you are on offense, signal for one shot, but take the shot with 15 seconds left. Show the attackers the bait again. They are in a hurry. They know you are going to give the pass from 1 to 2. They should cross mid-court with 10 to 12 seconds left. They have an idea of what they want to do to get the last shot. Therefore, 1 hurriedly passes to 2 as he sees the double-team approaching. X5 scores a lay-up on the interception. If you scored with 15 seconds left, the lay-up would make four straight unanswered points. If you are at home, the crowd is ecstatic and often victory is yours with a quarter still to play.

SHOW AND TELL

We show a stunt and make the offense tell us what they intend to do about it. From their reply our defense adjusts. We especially like to show and tell against teams that like to clear out. We call this stunt with the number 70.

1 passes in-bounds to 2 (Diagram 6-5). X2 shades 2 to the outside, forcing him toward the area cleared by 1. If 1 looped back into the outside lane occupied by 2, X2 would not want to channel 2 toward the area cleared by 1's cut downfloor. X1 would not be there to help. However, X2 would know this because X1 communicates to X2 his new location by the word "help," letting X2 know where to channel 2. So 2, if and when he dribbles, must dribble toward X1. Should 2 decide to throw a long pass, X3 would go for the interception while X1 would rotate back to cover 3. If the pass is complete, X3 covers 1 and X1 blankets 3.

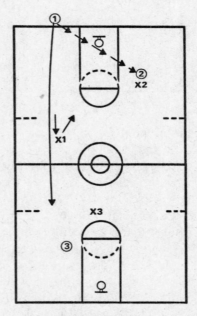

Diagram 6-5

As 1 clears out, X1 follows until 1 gets 25 or 30 feet away from 2. X1 then returns to an area about 20 feet away from 2, but in a position where he can see 1 should 1 decide to break back toward the ball. X3 gaps 1 and 3. That is, X3 plays between 1 and 3 where he can see both. X3 also stations himself at a good interception angle between the passer and 1. The pass must cover 30 feet or more. It must be at least semi-lobbed. Passing to either 1 or 3 offers a golden opportunity for an interception.

2 knows his coach has cleared an area for him to dribble into front court, but the defense did not cooperate. 2 also knows that a semi-lobbed pass of 30 feet can be intercepted. X2 encourages 2 to dribble. 2 sees X1 planning a stunt (run and jump switch or trap). 2 may plan to dribble toward X1 before reverse dribbling to the other outside lane and freeing himself. X2 knows this; but if X2 has mastered the proper containment principles of Chapter 1, he can control 2. X1 calls "jump" or "trap." When we call "70" from the bench, we expect X3 to get into the rotation. X4 and X5 can also get into the rotation. Or we can call "78," which we use to indicate to X3, X4, and X5 that we expect X1 and X2 to double-team 2 while X3, X4, and X5 cover a zone as in the numbering press (see Diagram 6-3).

We use "70" when offensive teams try to clear out for a good dribbler. We use "78" when the clearout man (1 in Diagram 6-5), loops to the lane just vacated by the dribbler as the dribbler begins his drive. "78" will also stop the dribble and split game (see Chapter 9). "78," by virtue of the trap by X1 and X2, halts the excellent dribbler from breaking free of the run and jump by keeping his dribble alive and looping (reverse dribbling) as he hears "jump."

TWO-ON-TWO STUNTS

When only two defenders press we eliminate the traps, running only the switches outlined in Chapter 2. This is the safest of all presses because there are three defenders near the defensive basket.

Double-teaming when the offense screens offers the only exception (Diagram 6-6). 2 moves toward X1, intending to set a screen on him, hoping to free 1 for a dribble into front court. But X2, who has postioned himself in the passing lane between 1 and 2, can reach X1 prior to 2. As 2 goes to set the screen, X2 double-teams 1 with X1. The two defenders can hold the double-team even after 2 cuts downfloor. Or when 2 leaves, an automatic "jump" can be called. This would rotate X1 onto 2 and leave X2 on 1.

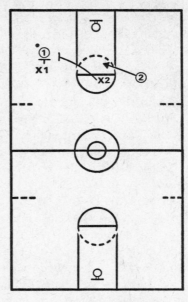

Diagram 6-6

If the offense suspects that the defense intends only a two-man press, they will not use screening maneuvers. They would probably clear out. X2 must not follow the clearout. He would follow until he gets about 20 feet away where he would wait for the dribbler.

Teams that have met our run and jump or one of our stunts against the dribbler unsuccessfully might be reluctant to dribble. They may set screens to free dribblers. We meet this offensive tactic by beating the screener to his point of screen. But if the screener beats us to the point of screen (because we were not alert), then we use the jump switch techniques described in Chapter 2.

Diagram 6-7 depicts a special two-on-two stunt. While X1 tries to channel 1 toward X2, 1 might have other ideas, especially if 1 has lost the ball on previous anti-dribbling stunts. 1 fakes inside and beats X1 on a dribble to the outside. 1 might be hesitant because of previous switches and traps. Downcourt teammates of X1 can help slow 1 down by hedging. X2 leaves 2 and sprints to get ahead of the dribble. Once X2 achieves a good angle, he cuts off 1. X1 has tried to maintain defense on 1. When X2 cuts off 1, 1 will probably pick up his dribble. X1, already in the passing lane between 1 and 2, jumps off to cover 2. X2 must yell "jump," keying X1 to get in the passing lane.

When we run two-on-two stunts, we use our two best pressers. They are responsible for the two men bringing the ball up the floor, even if one is a big man. We switch back when the opportunity presents itself in their half-court offense. Mismatches outside present no problems. Advantages outside go to the quicker not the bigger man.

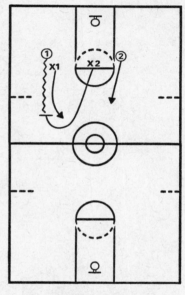

Diagram 6-7

THREE-ON-THREE STUNTS

All of our games find us opening in a three-man press: three against whatever. The offense, on many occasions, shows us the strategy and maneuvers they intend to use against our team presses, giving us an advantage in strategy: We can determine which press will neutralize their attack.

We can camouflage our three-man press, making it look like

a zone press. Often, teams show us their zone press attack which many use against our area man-to-man press (see Chapter 8).

Diagram 6-8 has the look of a drop-back zone press, but it is in fact a three-man press. Opponents attack with two guards in the holes. We like X1 to channel a dribbler down one side or another. For the sake of discussion, let's have X1 send 1 toward X2. When X2 wishes, he begins his run and jump maneuver, forcing 1 to pick up his dribble. X2 commands X1 by "jump" or "trap." X3 shades into the passing lane toward the poster, 3; but he mentally plays the passing lane to 4. X3 follows the pass. A pass to 4 would have X3 playing defense on 4, X1 defending 2, and X2 playing 1. 3 would be picked up by a deep defender. A pass to 2 would have X3 and X2 exchanging responsibilities.

This press slows the tempo around midcourt. Teams are reluctant to attack the two deep defenders, even if the pass is completed beyond X1, X2, and X3. 4 and 5, who usually receive the first pass, are not the top ball handlers. When they see the tandem defense of X4 and X5, they hold the ball before passing to 1 or 2 and getting into their half-court offense. Nothing is lost

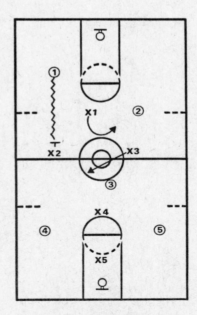

Diagram 6-8

by employing this press. Changing the game's tempo and some turnovers can be gained. This stunt is really the three-men-and-a-tandem dropped to midcourt.

This stunt can be combined with short-stopping and left field techniques described in Chapter 3. It can be run as a three-man face-guard press with a defender on the out-of-bounds passer. But when the ball is in-bounded, the three defenders retreat to the area between the 28-foot mark and the midcourt line.

These stunts and the three-man stunts discussed in Chapters 2 through 4 do not represent all possible three-man stunts. The number is limited only by the limits of the coach's mind.

FOUR-ON-FOUR STUNTS

All the three-man stunts will convert to four-man stunts. We call the fourth man the "react" man. He studies the third man, the gap shooter, and shoots the gap on the gap shooter's man when the gap shooter vacates his man to go after the trapper's man (the second defender). The fourth man reacts to the chain reaction. When the react defender rotates, musical chairs develop. All four defenders rotate to new assignments (see next chapter for more details).

We employ the fourth man when he is quick and when the offense brings down a fourth man to try to break our three-man press. We can still play short stop and left field on the in-bounds pass. Center field also becomes a possibility.

When we place four defenders in back court, we can run and jump team-wise, activate our area man-to-man press, or stunt from zone to man-to-man or from man-to-man to zone. We can face-guard out of a 1-2-1-1, the last man being the safety, and blitz trap or blitz switch on the in-bounds pass. The two defenders not involved can zone the passing lanes, giving the impression of a point zone press. Or the defender on the in-bounds passer can slide with his man to the free throw line, waiting for the in-bounds receiver to begin his dribble before running and jumping with a switch or a trap. We especially like to show zone then go man-to-man prior to activating our area man-to-man press (see Chapter 8).

The two-guard zone front stunts require that the first two defenders pick up the in-bounds receiver and the out-of-bounds passer. The other two defenders in the 2-2-1 look, the last man is the safety, must match up with the other two attackers.

Defensive players can face-guard out of the two-guard zone front. The two frontliners pick up the first two cutters. The defensive deep defender opposite the throw-in player picks up the third cutter toward the ball. The other defensive deep defender plays left field (see Chapter 3) until the pass is successfully in-bounded; then he picks up the in-bounds passer. We now have man-to-man coverage, ready to run one of the previously discussed stunts. We showed zone but went man-to-man.

Defensive teams can show man but go zone. This, too, can help confuse attacking teams. Defenders can accomplish this stunt by placing a defender on the out-of-bounds passer (1-2-1-1) or using a left fielder (2-2-1). Either way, the defenders can face-guard or they can permit an uncontested in-bounds pass.

If the man press goes into the 1-2-1-1 zone press, we want the immediate blitz trap on the in-bounds pass below the free throw line extended. A successful pass out of this trap ends the zone press. The trapper takes the passer. The container rotates to the open man. The two passing lane defenders should have the men that were stationed in those passing lanes.

If the man press goes into the 2-2-1 coverage, we do not blitz trap the in-bounds pass. We try to force the ball down the outside lane with the off-side front defender sinking deep into the middle lane. We force the dribble, allowing a deep defender to stop the ball around midcourt. This deep defender and the ball-side front defender double-team. The weakside deep defender rotates to a ball lane coverage and the weakside front defender covers the middle lane and the horizontal pass. The ball-side deep defender was the container, and as such must rotate to the open man if a successful pass comes out of the trap. The strongside frontliner stays with the passer. The weakside front defender takes the instant threat in the middle or horizontal lane, and the original weakside deep defender takes the attacker in the vertical ball-side lane.

Four-on-four stunts almost represent full team defensive play. Showing zone-going man has become popular. Showing zone-going man is difficult to attack. Showing man-going zone is equally perplexing. Alternating between the two can confuse even deliberate sophisticated attacks. And displaying both concepts prior to activating the area man-to-man press makes that press unsolvable.

7

Employing the
Run and Jump Press

All the stunts previously described can also be used in conjunction with the run and jump team press. The difference being that we can call the stunts by a separate signal; but if we activate our 100 press, the run and jump, the players become opportunists, stunting and running and jumping as the offense provides the opportunity.

You can make the run and jump an extension of your basic team defense, or you can use it as a different press. It becomes an extension when the players decide when to activate it while playing a basic team defense; and it becomes a separate press when you call it as you would any stunt.

This press, in other words, is an aggressive variation of our basic man-to-man defense. We can still face-guard the in-bounds pass. We can short-stop, left-field, and center-field. We can fan and funnel. We can blitz trap or blitz switch.

This press will distort and control our opponent's offense. If the opposition has a weak ball handler or a weak passer or a player who likes to pass off the dribble, the run and jump will force him to commit ball-handling errors. This press excites the defense, inspiring it to more and more interceptions, establishing a quicker game tempo.

Constant running of this press will compel the dribbler to make the obvious pass. The obvious pass is the one which is available when one defender leaves his man to establish the trap or switch. In the run and jump, the defensive rotation will frequently intercept the obvious pass or impel a longer pass, one easily intercepted. And one interception usually begets another.

After several interceptions of the obvious pass, attackers usually become aware of the team rotation and they will attempt to make a longer pass (beyond the gap shooter) to the attacker the gap shooter just left. This is the pass the defense had wanted the offense to attempt. The react man should intercept it.

Dribblers who become too wise will face another stunt before we run and jump again. So this press will work harmoniously with the other segments of this book.

Defensive players must possess aggressiveness and alertness to succeed at this press. But these are two qualities observed in all championship teams. A coach would not mind improving his team's aggressiveness and alertness, for all coaches want to win championships.

Late in the games that we are losing, our opponents will attempt to stall. But the gambling nature of this defense and its continuous rerunning can force delaying teams into hurried passes and can compel them out of the controlled pattern they are trying to use.

However, at the full court level, the defense is most effective. It creates chaos in a short time against inexperienced or undisciplined teams. Poor ball handlers and poor passers do not have a chance against the run and jump. And five small quick players, operating under the duress of a "catch-up" strategy, can cause the offense many problems as they try to in-bound the ball, advance it down the floor, or put it into play at half-court. Many otherwise lost games become victories with the run and jump.

MAJOR PRINCIPLES OF THE RUN AND JUMP

In all run and jump situations, the ball handler must be made to dribble. Then we want the trapper to impel the ball handler to kill his dribble. To accomplish this we activate the following postulates. You will notice that these axioms correspond to the principles of Chapter 5 and that they have already been drilled upon in the previous chapters. We present the laws here to draw the team press together. But where we previously presented a section and a drill, we will place in parentheses the location in the book of that section and that drill.

A. Container must control and turn the dribbler. The defender on the ball must make his man dribble. He can do this with loose or tight coverage. Tight coverage prevents the potential dribbler from finding an open receiver, while loose coverage invites the immediate dribble.

Most players in the back court look to dribble when they first receive the ball. Loose coverage would encourage this attacker to dribble. Some teams use a passing offense to attack all full court pressure. Tight coverage would prevent such teams from finding an open receiver, compelling the dribble (see **Zig-Zag Drill,** Chapter 1).

B. Container must contain the dribbler. After the player begins his dribble, the container must not be beaten by the dribbler. The container must channel the dribbler toward help. He should listen for the word "help." When he hears it, he knows a defensive teammate is in that area (see Channelling the Ball Handler, Chapter 1).

C. Trapper runs at outside shoulder. The dribbler must protect the ball with his body. This means he will always dribble with his outside hand (hand away from his defender). By running at his outside shoulder, the defender forces the dribbler to reverse, to dribble further outside, to pick up the ball, or to charge. The container would steal any crossover. The container should stop any inside move (see Run and Jump Switch and Trap, Chapter 2).

D. Distance for the run and jump. Distance is relative. It depends on how quickly the dribbler is moving: At a great speed, 20 feet may not be too great a distance; at a very slow, controlled speed, five feet may be too much.

The ideal distance is the smallest distance. Because we stay two-thirds the distance from the ball and one-third the distance from our man, we are only 12 to 13 feet away from the ball when our man is 20 feet from the ball. We never like to run and jump from a greater distance unless it is gambling time during the game. In fact, in front court the distance should be less—no greater than six to eight feet (see Proper Spacing, Chapter 5; and Floating, Chapter 2).

E. Talk. All defenders must talk. "Help" tells the defender on the ball where a trapper is. "Jump" orders the container to rotate. "Trap" asks the container to double-team before rotating (see Talking, Chapter 1). Unless we have called "fan," we prefer for our run and jumps to occur on the inside, and we prefer that they occur after a reverse dribble. Funnelling combined with our area man-to-man press can destroy offenses (see Chapter 8).

F. Hedging. This is a defensive fake. A trapper acts as if he intends to run and jump, but he merely fakes a step or two before coming back to his own man. This must be called. Otherwise, a gap shooter or a react man might be moving to cover the hedger's assigned man. To avoid confusing these defenders, we call hedging (see Hedging, Chapter 2).

G. Kill the looper. Many dribblers will keep the ball alive by reverse dribbling to break free from the run and jump switch. When this strategy starts to hurt the press, we run and jump trap or we activate the area man-to-man press (see Traps and Switching, Chapter 4; also see Chapter 8).

H. Making a commitment. Once a trapper begins his run and jump switch or trap, he must race hard and fast with no hesitation. He has told his teammates that he has begun a stunt. Gap shooters and react men must begin their movement as the trapper starts his. This way we have the team acting in concert, acting as one instead of five. When the gap shooter or react defenders commit, they must race hard, never hesitating and never turning back (see Double-Teaming and Shooting the Gaps, Chapter 2).

I. Anticipate. Gap shooters, react men, and goalies must remain alert. They must anticipate trappers activating the run and jump. They could possibly leave their men before the trapper leaves his. They must not be afraid to gamble (see Developing Anticipation, Chapter 1).

Gap shooters, react men, and goalies can see the direction of the dribble. This should enable them to anticipate and begin moving toward the interception earlier.

J. A team defense. Because this is a team press and not a two- or three-man stunt, all the principles of Chapter 5 must be honored at all times. We never want the press begun until all five defenders are above the ball. And we never want a dribbler to penetrate freely into the area below the defensive foul lane (see Chapter 5 for all the team principles).

DRILLS TO TEACH THE RUN AND JUMP

Before we teach the five-on-five team press, we build our full court defense with a two-on-two, three-on-three, and three-on-two drill. These are also stunts. The two-on-two stunt is developed by the two guards pressing the two men bringing the ball up the court (Diagram 7-1). The defender away from the dribbler races over to cover the vacated attacker. The three-on-three drill (Diagram 7-2) involves the same original move but a different rotation: As the defender away from the dribbling guard races toward the dribbler, the defensive forward comes up to cover the open offensive guard and the dribbler's original defender rotates to the vacated attacking forward. The three-on-two stunt (Diagram 7-3) is used to stop two exceptionally talented ball handlers from advancing the ball. Using these stunts, any bad pass can be picked off and any completed pass can still be covered man-to-man.

Two-on-Two Run and Jump Drill

Procedure (Diagram 7-1):

1. Line players up in two lines. The offense advances the ball downcourt and back; then we rotate from offense to defense to the end of the line.
2. 1 dribbles but X1 will not let him outside. 2 may never get above 1. X2 may never get below the line of the advancement of the ball.
3. When X2 wants, he runs directly at 1 as X1 forces inside. If 1 continues his dribble, he must charge X2 or veer outside. If he veers outside, X1 continues his pressure and X2 helps. If 1 picks up the ball to pass to 2, X2 tries to deflect it as X1 races to cover 2, and we continue this run and jump the length of the court and back. If X1 and

X2 steal the ball, they fast-break. X1 and X2 hold their double-team as long as 1 continues his dribble. If 1 and 2 cross, X1 and X2 can switch, creating the impression of a zone press.

Objectives:

1. To teach the defenders how to play run and jump defense.
2. To condition the athlete for pressure defense and fast-break offense.
3. To improve offensive ball handling.

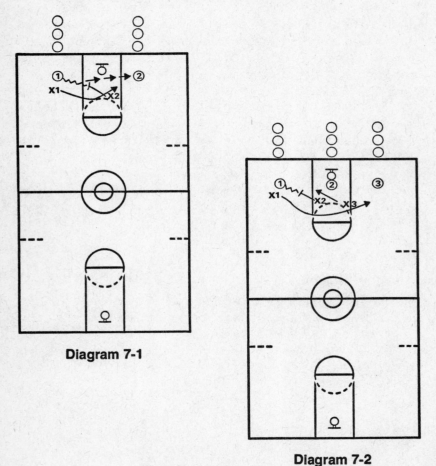

Diagram 7-1

Diagram 7-2

Three-on-Three Run and Jump Drill

Procedure (Diagram 7-2):

1. Line players up in three lines. The offense advances the ball downcourt and back; then we rotate from offense to defense to the end of the line.
2. If 2, the center player, is dribbling, he must be going toward either 1 or 3. In either case, that is a two-on-two run and jump (see Diagram 7-1). However, if either 1 or 3 is dribbling, we force him to the inside and run our three-on-three run and jump.
3. For the sake of discussion, let's have 1 drive to the inside and run our three-man run and jump. As 1 drives inside, X2 races toward 1 and double-teams with X1 until 1 puts both hands on the ball. This is X1's cue to race hard to cover 3. Meanwhile, X3 has shot the gap between 1 and 2 for the interception. Even if the pass is completed, we are still in a man-to-man press: X1 on 3, X2 on 1, and X3 on 2. And, if the offense should turn the ball over the defense can fast-break. The coach should require that the two offensive men without the ball stay behind the advancement of the ball. That not only expedites teaching, but it permits more run and jumps per possession.

Objectives:

1. To teach three defensive men how to coordinate their efforts in a three-man run and jump.
2. To improve offensive ball handling.
3. To teach proper methods of double-teaming.
4. To teach shooting the gap.
5. To condition defensive players for full court pressure.

Three-on-Two Run and Jump Drill

Procedure (Diagram 7-3):

1. Line players up in two lines. The offense advances the ball downcourt and back. X3 starts at safety on the way downcourt and X1 starts at safety on the way back. X2 is the first safety when the two lines rotate after a trip downfloor and back.

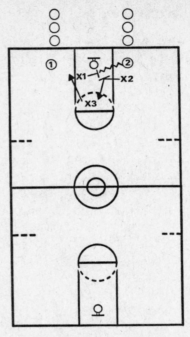

Diagram 7-3

2. X1 and X2 run and jump switch or trap while X3 shoots the gap. After X1 and X2 stop 2's dribble, X2 drops and becomes the new short safety, waiting to shoot the gap on the next run and jump.

Objectives:

1. To teach three defenders how to run and jump against two attackers.
2. To condition defensively for full court pressure.
3. To teach double-teaming and shooting the gap.
4. To improve the ball handlers offensively.

RESPONSIBILITIES OF THE CONTAINER

The container, in our vernacular, names the man guarding the ball handler. His first duty is to make the ball handler put the ball on the floor. He can force this dribble by playing tight or by playing loose. We prefer pressure because the dribbler cannot easily find a potential pass receiver while he is trying to protect the ball from his defender.

Regardless of the decision of whether to play tight or loose, this defender must control the dribbler. He must turn the dribbler toward a helping teammate. He would know where his teammate was because his partners would be yelling "help," "help," "help." He must also contain this dribbler, never permitting him to escape.

As the trapper approaches the container, the container should see him or sense his presence. This is a time of great escape for the dribbler. The container must make sure the ball handler does not penetrate through the area between the trapper and the container. The container, not the trapper, has the responsibility of preventing this split.

The container must also remain alert to the possibility of the dribbler reversing his dribble back in the direction from whence he came. When the attacker does reverse dribble, the container should momentarily help the trapper control the dribbler even if a jump has been called. He would not be responsible for this move, however, unless the trapper yelled "trap."

When the trapper yells "trap," the container and the trapper double-team the ball. The container is responsible for the split and the looping action (reverse dribble) toward the outside, from the direction that the dribbler has just come. The trapper prevents the dribbler from escaping to the outside in the direction the dribbler is going. If the dribbler picked up his dribble, the trapper might require the container to find the open attacker immediately. The word "used" sends the container on the fish hook route. Otherwise, the container leaves when the dribbler passes out of the trap.

When the trapper yells "jump" or "used," the container turns his head to the inside of the court to find the open man as he begins to run his fish hook route. When he spots that open attacker, he must turn his head down the passing lane between the passer and the potential receiver. He must quickly and accurately adjust his path so that he can get his body in the passing lane of the two offensive players. Containers should look for and expect this "obvious" pass.

Should a pass be completed to this obvious receiver, the container is again the defender on the ball—with container's duties again. But should the original container prevent this pass, he now becomes a trapper, a gap shooter, or a react man.

When the obvious pass is completed, the container must again control, turn, and contain his new attacker. He must not permit the dribbler to escape downfloor.

If the obvious pass is not made out of the run and jump switch, the container accepts his responsibilities in two ways. If the dribbler picked up his dribble, all defenders, including the ex-container, must get into full denial position between the passer, who has no escape but to pass, and the potential pass receivers. Many times this dribble "used" drill forces a bad pass, a ten-second violation, or a held ball (if the run and jump occurred in front court).

A dribble kept alive, like a successful pass out of the run and jump switch, would require the ex-container to assume a help position: to get proper spacing, to mentally play the passing lane, and so on. And the process begins again.

RESPONSIBILITIES OF THE TRAPPER

The trapper is the defender who runs directly at the outside shoulder of the dribbler, shouting "jump" or "trap."

All trappers begin from help position. They should wait until the dribbler comes within 10 to 15 feet, and they would want the dribbler to be advancing toward them. When these two conditions exist, we want the trapper to run at the outside shoulder of the dribbler. The container would steal the dribble if the ball was being handled with the inside hand. The trapper attacks the ball low, urging the ball handler to pick up his dribble.

If the dribbler chooses to keep his dribble alive, he must do one of four things. He can continue in the line he is driving. This would result in a charge into the trapper, an offensive violation. He can try to split the two defenders, the container and the trapper. To successfully complete this offensive move, the dribbler would have to change the ball over from the outside hand to the inside hand. As the changeover occurs, the container should steal the dribble. The container also has perfect positioning to draw the charge.

The dribbler has two other avenues available. Faking a dribble inside and driving around the outside gives him a third and a fourth option. He can reverse dribble, going back toward his starting point. Or, he can fake inside and drive directly outside. If the trapper has called "trap," then the container must not allow the dribbler to escape with a reverse dribble. The trapper must not let the dribbler have the outside in a continuing dribble. Both defenders can help against the split, but it remains the primary responsibility of the container.

If the trapper has called "jump," then he becomes a container. He must control, turn, and contain the dribbler, regardless of the direction the dribbler chooses. The trapper—now container—must turn the dribbler toward help.

Run and jumps work best when the trapper startles the dribbler. The two best times to surprise him are when he reverses and starts in a new direction and when he is preoccupied with trying to defeat his own defender who is offering excellent pressure. In the first case, the attacker cannot see the entire court. He has his back to his downcourt teammates. In the second case, he must concentrate so much on protection of the dribble that he limits his own view. In both cases, the obvious pass usually follows the astonished dribbler.

Once the trapper commits himself to run at the dribbler, he must not hesitate; he must go and go hard. He must never turn back. Although the trapper knows his own intentions and the container reacts only to the trapper's beckon, the other three defensive teammates of the trapper would become confused if the trapper raced toward the dribbler and then suddenly turned back. They would not know when to shoot the gap or when to react. The gap shooter, for example, reads the trapper and reacts instantly to the trapper's decision. Therefore, the trapper must show no indecision.

Trappers call "trap" or "jump." They can also call "used" when the dribbler picks up his dribble. It is best to jump when the obvious pass is being made or when the dribbler will pick up his dribble. But when the dribbler continues his dribble, the trap is better. A completed pass out of the trap would still mandate the jump rotation.

DUTIES OF THE GAP SHOOTER

Diagram 7-4 depicts a typical run and jump situation involving a trapper, X2, a container, X1, and a gap shooter, X3. As the diagram shows, X3 begins in a help position. He is a floater and should sag properly. He plays his man physically and the passing lane mentally. He should see the trapper, X2, clearly.

When the gap shooter sees the trapper leave his man, the gap shooter must also leave his. They should depart simultaneously. X3 knows if 1 is dribbling toward X2, and he knows that X2 will probably activate a run and jump. That knowledge allows the gap shooter to anticipate the trapper's departure. A fan or funnel call would give the gap shooter another step or two edge.

Trappers and gap shooters should move together, as though they were tied to each other. And even if the gap shooter knows he has no chance for an interception, he must go if we have a three-, four-, or five-man rotation called.

Should a pass be completed to his new man, 2 in Diagram 7-4, the gap shooter would assume the duties of a container.

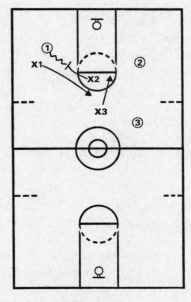

Diagram 7-4

Should a pass be completed to a different attacker, the gap shooter becomes a trapper, a react man, or another gap shooter.

If the dribble has been killed and the trapper has yelled "trap" (let's let 1 pick up his dribble in Diagram 7-4), the gap shooter can possibly zone two passing lanes (the lane between 1 and 2 and the lane between 1 and 3). So the coach can create a three-on-three drill to teach zone press coverage of the passing lanes. If the trapper had shouted "jump," X3 would cover 2, X2 would contain 1, and X1 would rotate to the open man, 3. In either case, a completed pass would impel the process to begin again.

DUTIES OF THE REACT MAN

Where the gap shooter indicates the third man in the team defensive rotation, the react man specifies the fourth. This defender can be on the ball side or the weakside.

When the react man is on the ball side, we prefer for him to contest the vertical pass and let only the weakside rotate (Diagram 7-5). But we still give him freedom of choice. The container must read his teammate's reaction to determine if his rotation is three deep or more.

X4, the react man, must make a choice: Deny 4 the ball or get into the rotation. His decision can depend upon 1's previous reaction to an earlier run and jump; We prefer denial, but we do not demand it.

When the react man is on the weakside and we have a team rotation called, we expect him to shoot the gap on the lane between the passer and the man the gap shooter just left. X4, in Diagram 7-6, represents a weakside react man shooting the gap on 3, the gap shooter's original man. X1, the container, fish hooks to the open man (4 in Diagram 7-6).

React men leave their assigned player at the exact moment that the gap shooter leaves his. This makes a simultaneous four-man musical chair rotation. Depending upon where the ball moves after the initial trap or jump (by a successful pass or by a continued dribble), the react man would rotate to become a container, a trapper, a gap shooter, or another react man. From there, the process begins again.

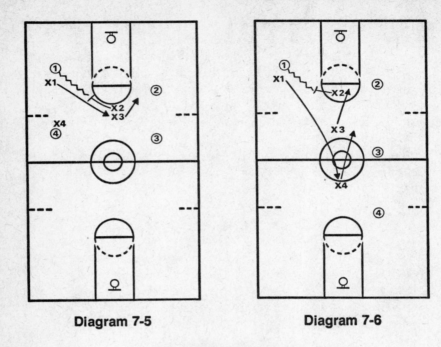

Diagram 7-5   Diagram 7-6

DUTIES OF THE GOALIE

Goalies defend their defensive goal. They jealously guard it, rotating from it only when they see that a teammate can cover for them.

Diagram 7-7 shows the goalie, X5, not becoming involved in the rotation. Goalies should carefully consider involvement in the rotation when the gap they will be shooting is in the back court. In Diagram 7-7, the goalie would have had to cover 4 (if X4 becomes a react man) or 3, both of whom are located in back court. He should, as the diagram indicates, ignore rotation plans unless the defensive team has called a five-man rotation.

Diagram 7-8 shows 4 in the front court. Should X4 become a react man, then X5, the goalie, can consider shooting the gap between the passer, 1, and the potential receiver, 4. X5 must leave when X4 leaves. He must not hesitate, clearly indicating to X1 his proper rotation along his fish hook trail. All five defenders play musical chairs to new assignments. A completed pass or a continued dribble would impel the process to begin again.

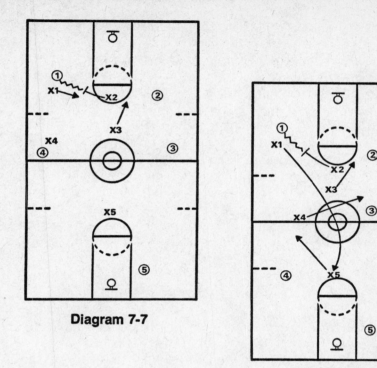

Diagram 7-7

Diagram 7-8

PLAYS INVOLVING THE RUN AND JUMP

Coaches can call each run and jump as to the area of the surprise and the number of players involved. Coaches can follow any completed pass out of the run and jump switch or trap into a zone press or a man-to-man press. In other words, they can use the run and jump to stunt from man-to-man into man-to-man, or they can use the run and jump to stunt from man-to-man into a zone press. All of these opportunities will be covered in detail in the next chapter on the area man-to-man press.

At this time, we want to teach our players to react to offensive situations. We want them to think and to control the game using a team pressing technique with little or no help from the bench. The players must learn to read the offensive intentions and to react to them.

Coaches can make the run and jump completely free-lance defensive thinking by letting the players decide when to activate it. It can, under those conditions, be an extension of the basic team defense. Or, the coach can make it a separate defense and call it from the bench.

However, even under free-lance defensive thinking, coaches can still decide what they want from their players. For example, they can allow only a certain number of men to run and jump. Or, they can dictate that they want a run and jump to occur only under certain offensive conditions. The remainder of this chapter will cover those offensive situations. The first four chapters covered not only the fundamentals of pressing, but the stunts using only a certain number of players. The next chapter will combine the two into the ultimate press: the area man-to-man press.

ATTACKING THE REVERSE DRIBBLE

The best time to run and jump occurs as the dribbler reverses his direction. His view downcourt is minimal; so we try to force the reverse dribble as often as possible. Plus, we want to always be alert to the offense initiating the reverse dribble without the defense compelling it.

Dribblers aid off-of-the-ball defenders in their coverage. When a dribbler drives away from a gap shooter, react man, or goalie, these defenders can begin sagging off their men and toward the dribbler. These off-of-the-ball defenders, however, must use good judgment. They must always be in a position to prevent the direct return pass.

We develop our defensive attack against the reverse dribble in three ways: trap, give the outside then take it away, and follow the loop dribble by forcing a second change of direction.

Attackers who try to escape the run and jump by repeatedly reverse dribbling out of the jump end up being trapped. In other words, if we are being hurt by dribblers who are constantly reverse dribbling, we tell the trapper not to call "jump" but to call "trap." This puts two defenders on the ball handler. We can zone the passing lanes; or we can cover all but one attacker man-to-man, hoping the passer cannot find the open receiver. Any successful pass out of the run and jump trap can be followed by a rotation into either man-to-man coverage or zone coverage.

If we call "jump" and the offensive dribbler loops (reverse dribbles) out of it, we force a second change of direction, followed by another jump or a trap (Diagram 7-9). X2 runs at 1, yelling "jump," sending X1 to cover 2. Wherever 2 goes, X1 will not follow if we have called the second change of direction stunt, or if we intend to free-lance and X1 knows what X2 is attempting. Of course, another defender could have shot the gap on the initial jump by X2; therefore, that defender would have the duties of X1. Diagram 7-9 does not show another defender because we want to keep the illustration as simple as possible. After yelling "jump" and seeing 1 reverse dribble out of the jump, X2 must race to the outside of 1. Defensive teammates of X2 can help bring 1 under control by hedging and retreating, hedging and retreating. X2 wants to allow sufficient distance between himself and 1 so that 1 will not crossover dribble to escape from X2. Once X2 establishes good position, 1 will reverse dribble again. X1 has anticipated this and is coming hard to trap (if we have a possible ten-second violation) or jump (if we

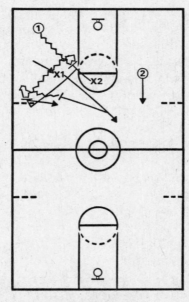

Diagram 7-9

think 1 will now pick up his dribble). Many offensive teams do not plan for a second potential pass, do not drill on attacking the second trap, making it easier to intercept a pass after the second jump or trap.

Instead of the defense permitting the offense to call the reverse dribble, the defense can compel the offense to reverse dribble. We call this giving the outside and then taking it away. It was discussed in detail in Chapter 4. The last half of Diagram 7-9 also illustrates this stunt. In fact, Diagram 7-9 is a combination of a funnelled run and jump switch followed immediately by a give-the-outside-then-take-it-away maneuver (both discussed fully in Chapter 4).

ATTACKING THE CLEAROUT

Complete clearouts would eliminate the defensive run and jump. No trapper could locate in back court if all of the off-the-ball defenders followed their assigned men into front court.

When teams clear out, man-to-man defensive coaches must adjust minutely. Defenders can be instructed not to follow their men into front court. Such defenders should follow their men until they are about 30 feet away (the defender would be about 20 feet away). Then the defender should pause, waiting for the ball handler to dribble before activating a run and jump. Up-court defensive teammates of the trapper and container can anticipate a few steps further and become better gap shooters.

Funnelling offers a defensive gem. All defenders know the dribbler will drive inside. All can anticipate and gain a few steps on the attackers. When funnelling techniques are used, inside defenders on guard clearouts must stop 20 feet away from the ball.

Blitz traps (traps on the in-bounds pass receiver) provide an excellent defense of the clearout. The other three defenders can zone the passing lanes or they can become gap shooters, react men, or goalies.

Or, they can let the in-bounds pass receiver's defender and the defender on the out-of-bounds passer begin with a two-man run and jump. Then, on a second run and jump, the entire team can get into the rotation (Diagram 7-10).

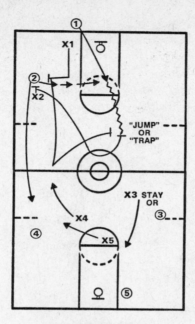

Diagram 7-10

X1 and X2 defend 1 and 2. An immediate blitz trap forces 2 to pass back to 1. Now, 2 instead of 1 must clear out. The offense had wanted 1 to pass to 2 and 1 to clear out. So now the defense has forced a different offensive player to handle the ball. 1 will see his opening and probably begin to dribble immediately, which is what the defense wants. This eliminates 2's attempt to completely clear out. X2 must race hard to reachieve positioning on 1 for the second run and jump. Or, another defender may have become a gap shooter on 1's reception of the pass from 2. In that case X2 would run the fish hook. However, for the sake of simplicity, in the diagram we will let X2 cut off 1. A third thing now favors the defense: The ball has advanced further downcourt, making the area from the gap shooter to the passing lane between 1 and the obvious pass receiver, 2, much less, giving the gap shooter a better opportunity to intercept. A fourth blessing for the defense: The ball is being dribbled while the clearout is occurring.

On the second jump or trap, X4 should pick off the pass to 2. X5 can zone between 5 and 4, or he can take 4. If it is a trap,

X3 should contest the strongside receiver, 3, leaving 5 as X2's man. If it is a jump, X3 could stay or go. If he goes, X2's new attacker would be 3.

Zone presses would eliminate the clearout, but this book contains only man-to-man ideas. And the best defensive strategy (zone or man) to eliminate clearouts remains the area man-to-man press (see Chapter 8).

ATTACKING THE LONG PASS OFFENSE

Long passes can be intercepted. The defense wants the offense to throw the long pass.

Coaches must insist that all five defenders begin retreating while the ball is in the air. They must sprint hard to recover because all defenders must always be ahead of the ball (a cardinal principle, Chapter 5).

Let's illustrate a long cross-court pass and a long vertical pass. Diagrams 7-11 and 7-12 will suffice to show our coverage.

1 passes cross-court to 4 (Diagram 7-11). This pass of 50 feet or more should never be completed. X1 must pressure the ball handler. If X1 can compel the dribble, the long pass threat is further reduced. X5, the defender below the receiver, decides instantly on a steal, a charge (if 4 is moving toward X5), or pressuring 4 (if 4 can successfully receive the ball). But X5 must go, assuming the duties of a trapper. The off-side defender, X3, has plenty of time to rotate to 5. X4 tries to deflect the long pass. X4 undertakes the container's role and rotates to the open man, 3. X1 and X2 must race hard to get above the ball. If the pass is successful, X5 must pressure 4, keeping him from immediately finding 5 or 3.

Diagram 7-12 displays the long vertical pass coverage. X1 pressures the passer, hoping for the dribble. X3 goes for the interception or the deflection. X5, the deepest defender, reads and reacts. X5 should gain an interception, draw a charge, or pressure 3 after a completion. X4, the off-side defender, must cover the attacker near the basket. X1 and X2 race upcourt to get ahead of the ball.

X5 is the key to long pass defense. If he does his job, he can delay the offense even if the pass is successful. Any delay and the full defense can recover. Because of this, the three deep defend-

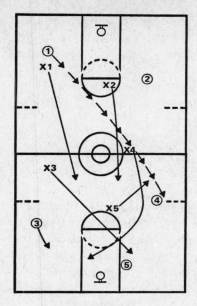

Diagram 7-11

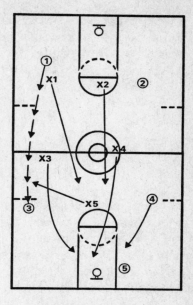

Diagram 7-12

ers can gamble. And because of their run and jump rotation, they should eliminate any open passing lane. X1 is also a key. If he can force a higher arc, the downcourt defenders will have more time to rotate.

An easy teaching point: The deepest defender becomes the trapper; the defender on the receiver becomes the container. Therefore, the rotation does not change.

A long pass completion to the deepest receiver, 5, would result in a lay-up. But this is the hardest pass to complete under pressure, one not often attempted.

ATTACKING WITH ONE GAP SHOOTER

When one gap shooter becomes involved, the pressure end of the defense has only three members. That implies that two defenders protect the defensive basket in either a gap or a tandem configuration. We often begin games with only three men involved in the rotation and two concerned with basket defense.

When left for the players to decide, there are more two-man run and jumps than three-man. There are more three-man rotations than four. In fact, there are few four-man rotations and almost no five-man rotations during any game. But there should always be a third man involved when the obvious pass receiver is moving away from the passer.

Fortunately, we have devised a system where we can call the number of men we want rotating (see Chapter 8). Our system also will allow the players to decide.

ATTACKING WITH A GAP SHOOTER AND A REACT MAN

These four defenders can decide simultaneously to activate a four-man rotation, or we can call it from the bench. Usually, when we call a four-man rotation, we utilize our area man-to-man press. With the area press we have the added dimension of employing a zone, by either showing zone going man, showing zone going zone, or showing man going zone.

A coach can establish principles for his defenders to follow if he prefers them to read and to react. For example, the coach can decree that only players on the off-side can become involved in the rotation. This would mean that strongside defenders would play denial, eliminating them from the musical chairs of the run and jump. This also aids the container in his running of the fish hook.

ATTACKING WITH A FULL ROTATION

Full rotations, in our belief, should have a guiding principle. Because full rotations take the goalie away from the goal, another defender must be retreating to the area of the basket. This defender must leave as the goalie leaves.

Few opportunities, under the players' free-lance defensive thinking, will present themselves for a full rotation. But we help the defenders decide with two guiding axioms or teaching points. These tenets correspond with our long pass defense. We stress: They are teaching points, not rules. They are something to go by, not something that must be followed.

A goalie may rotate to any weakside attacker any time that weakside attacker's defender leaves him. But when the goalie rotates under this condition, we insist upon the strongside defender rotating to the goalie position. For example, in Diagram 7-7, X5 could react to X3's movement. When X5 reacts, X4 must rotate and become the goalie. In other words, when the deepest defender becomes a react man, then the deepest defender on the strongside must rotate to the deepest defender's man.

A goalie may also rotate to any attacker located in front court. Diagram 7-8 depicts such a rotation.

These two teaching points have enabled us to free-lance a five-man rotation without conceding the lay-up. They also correspond with the goalie's coverage in our area man-to-man press (see next chapter).

8

Coaching the
Area Man-to-Man Press

Just beyond the run and jump press lies the area man-to-man press. Like the run and jump press, the area press is a man-to-man press. But the area press can run the full gamut: It can show zone go zone, show zone go man, show man go zone, or show man go man. The area press can make use of face-guarding, short-stopping, left-fielding, or center-fielding. The area press utilizes the run and jump switch or trap, the blitz switch or trap, and the give-the-outside-then-take-it-away techniques. The area press is limitless.

During these times when coaches stress transition, the area press blends perfectly. It is the defense of the future.

Many modern defensive coaches feel it is impossible to stop a good offensive player one-on-one. So, two-on-one and three-on-one defensive tactics must be planned; and it is safer to employ two-on-one and three-on-one methods 90 feet away from your defensive basket than it is to engage in such defensive strategy when only 20 feet away.

By teaching the area press, you can dictate the tempo of the game. You can even tell the offensive coach what maneuvers you will permit him to perform.

The area press forces mistakes, reducing the offensive efficiency of the attackers and hence giving the defenders a better chance of winning. When the attackers finally get a good shot, they frequently rush it, missing it. It can become quite a maze for an offensive team to negotiate.

Only very well-conditioned teams can effectively run the press. Practicing the drills as well as the complete press daily will condition your team and keep it conditioned. Because it scores many points, the area press can be considered an offense.

Many of the area stunts are not gambles. They can be run at little or no risk. However, the area press can become a gambling press if the game situation demands it.

Starting the game with a safe stunt impels our players to get into motion, a great aid to offense as well as defense. This defense teaches thinking, savvy, and concentration—three qualities evident in all championship teams.

Coaches who believe only in zone pressure will love the area press. Those coaches can show man and go zone or show zone and go zone. They can go from the area press into their favorite zone press.

By teaching the area man-to-man press, you will have taught your players to attack a man press, a zone press, a fast break, and a defense of the fast break. In other words, you will have taught your players the transition game.

RULES OF THE AREA MAN-TO-MAN PRESS

All the principles of Chapter 5 must be taught first because they are the backbone to all presses, both zone and man. The area man-to-man press has eight postulates of its own. Each will be fully explained in this section. Each will be mentioned where applicable throughout this chapter. Each will work in harmony with the principles of Chapter 5.

1. When a defender pressures the out-of-bounds passer, other defenders rotate counterclockwise. For the sake of discussion, we will begin explaining the area man-to-man press from a 2-2-1 alignment (Diagram 8-1). X1 and X4 would occupy the ball lane, X2 and X3 patrol the middle lane, and X5 is the goalie. Each defender has an area, and each defender has the attacker located in that area. If there is no attacker in his area, the defender floats to a deeper area until he visually contacts his man. If two offensive players overload one area, the front attacker becomes the responsibility of the defender upcourt and the back attacker is the deeper defender's man.

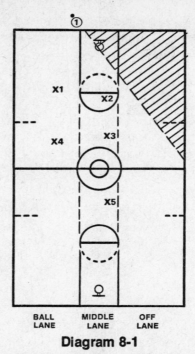

Diagram 8-1

We leave the off lane uncovered, hoping for a lob pass to that area. A pass we frequently intercept.

The shaded area can easily be covered by X2. Any pass to that region must be bounced, because the backboard would deflect any semi-lobbed pass. X2 knows this and uses it to his advantage when playing the passing lanes. X2, when playing the passing lanes, can play denial or he can open to the ball. He can alternate his coverage.

Many defensive strategies, such as face-guard, present themselves to this alignment, including guarding the out-of-bounds passer. If we decide to put pressure on the passer, 1 in Diagram 8-1, we rotate our defensive assignments counterclockwise. Because most teams take the ball out of the basket and immediately check the lane to their right (ball lane in Diagram 8-1), we want that lane covered quickly. X1 would face-guard the first attacker there. X2 would cover 1, the out-of-bounds passer. X3 would have the middle and the off lane. X4 would rotate into the middle lane, playing center field. Not only would X1, under this rule, have immediate coverage on the first obvious receiver (85 percent of the time the ball is in-bounded here), but X3 would rotate into the second obvious passing lane for the interception of the bounce pass to the middle or the off-ball lane.

X3 should play denial, not face-guard defense. X3 could open to the ball. He has the backboard to help him.

This rule switches the zone look. What began as a 2-2-1 alignment has suddenly become a 1-2-1-1 array. But the area press need not stay zone. It can revert back to man as the pass is in-bounded.

2. When face-guard pressuring, there is an automatic two-man run and jump when ball is tossed over the front attacker's head. Diagram 8-2 depicts face-guard coverage and pressure on the out-of-bounds passer. If there were no pressure on the out-of-bounds passer, the rotation after 2 in-bounds the ball would still be the same. X4, the short safety, lines up in a direct downcourt line with the passer. If the passer runs the baseline, which he may if there has been no violation, X4 runs along with him. This keeps X4 in a better position to intercept a lob pass. This also keeps him in a perfect position to run and jump any in-bounds completion. We teach this coverage in a drill.

Procedure (Diagram 8-2):

1. X2 covers 2. X1 and X3 face-guard while X4 covers short safety.
2. As 2 passes in-bounds, X2 yells "ball." This tells X1 and X3 to try to deflect any lob pass, to steal any direct pass, or to rotate to a new position if a pass is successfully in-bounded. In Diagram 8-2, 1 has faked X1 and received the ball in-bounds in front of him. X2 can blitz trap, or he can sink into the middle lane to continue the area man-to-man press.
3. X1 covers the receiver, 1, with containment defense. X2 races toward the free throw line in the middle lane, always getting above the ball. X3 covers the deep portion of the ball lane.
4. A coach could use a blitz trap to switch defensive coverage from a man to a zone, from a man to a man, from a zone to a man, and from a zone to a zone.

Objectives:

1. To teach face-guard pressing out of the area man-to-man press.
2. To teach players to react as the ball is thrown in-bounds.
3. To teach defenders to get to their new areas after the ball is in-bounded in front of the face-guarders.
4. To teach defenders how to rotate coverage from man to zone, from zone to man, from man to man, and from zone to zone.

Diagram 8-3 describes the reactions of the defenders when the ball is passed over the heads of the face-guarding defenders. We also teach this recovery in a drill.

Procedure (Diagram 8-3):

1. X2 covers 2. X1 and X3 face-guard while X4 covers short safety.
2. X2 yells "ball" as 2 passes in-bounds. If X1 can deflect the pass, we have a chance for recovering. X3, playing denial instead of face-guard in the off lane, can see the

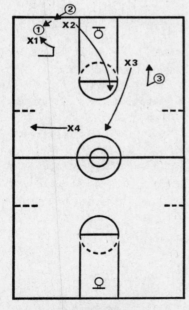

Diagram 8-2

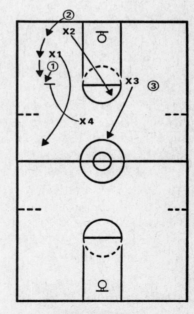

Diagram 8-3

in-bounds pass. Instantly, X3 races to defend his new position. If X1 has deflected the in-bounds pass toward the middle of the court, X3 has an excellent chance to recover it.

3. X4 responds to the in-bounds pass. If he can deflect or intercept it, we want him to do so. If not, he should have instant coverage on 1, preventing any quick movement or pass downcourt. X2 and X3 should have recovered to their new areas. X1 and X4 operate under the two-man run and jump rules. If X4 wants a trap or a jump, he calls it. If nothing is called, X1 automatically jumps. We pre-fer a jump if there is a deeper ball lane attacker; a trap if there is none.

4. Traps can change the defense from man to zone as well as from man to man. This drill can be used to teach such coverage.

Objectives:

1. To teach face-guard pressing out of the area man-to-man press.
2. To teach players to react to the command "ball."
3. To teach defenders how to get to their new positions when the ball is thrown over the head of a face-guarding defender.
4. To teach defenders to go from man to zone, from man to man, from zone to zone, and from zone to man.

3. *Defense of clearout cutters.* Clearout cutters can break between their defenders and the ball (middle cut), or they can cut behind their defenders (backdoor). We have a rule that gov-erns the coverage on each.

We divide the full court into four areas (Diagram 8-4). 40 represents the area between the free throw line and our offen-sive basket, the area where we face-guard. 30 covers the region between the free throw line and the 28-foot marker. 20 de-scribes the district from the 28-foot marker to half-court. And 10 is from half-court to the defensive 28-foot marker.

A. *If a middle cut or a cut in the middle lane is used, the middle lane defenders exchange responsibilities.* Diagram 8-5 shows a give-and-go, a form of a middle cut. If this cut occurs in the middle lane, we have the off-ball or middle lane defenders exchange responsibilities. The reasoning is simple: A pass to any attacker in the middle lane breaks the press, and X1 has a better chance to keep 1 from posting. So X4 comes to the middle lane front where he can activate a stunt.

When 1 passed to 2, all the defenders would be moving toward the pass (Diagram 8-5). This should place X2 on the ball, X3 in the ball lane, X1 in fronting coverage of 1's cut, and X4 playing any lob pass to 1 as X4 moves to the front. When X1 reaches an area 30 removed from the ball (from 40 into 10, for example), he returns to help play the deep position in the area man-to-man press. When X1 crosses into an area 20 removed from the ball (for example, from 40 into 20), X4 slides into an up position in the area man-to-man press.

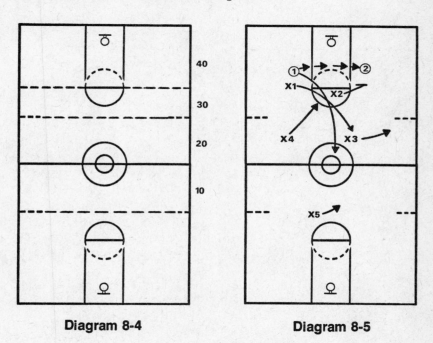

| Diagram 8-4 | Diagram 8-5 |

B. If a backdoor cut is used, carry the attacker to the deep defender and then return to your area. Diagram 8-6 illustrates this coverage. 1 passes to 2 and breaks backdoor in the off-ball lane. X1 follows until he can release him to X4. However, we do not want X1 to go farther than 20 away (from 40 into 20). X4's

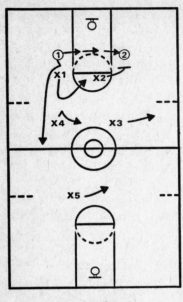

Diagram 8-6

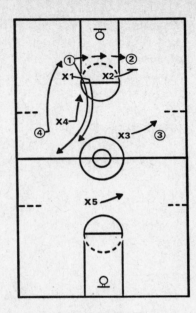

Diagram 8-7

man may have located deeper; therefore, X4 may be deeper. If so, X1 must wait until X4 can come up to cover 1 before he can release him and return to an area only 10 away from the ball (40 into 30).

During either of these cuts, X2 must pressure 2, preventing him from easily spotting an open receiver. We want 2 to dribble. But if 2 keeps his poise and does not dribble, we want his pass lobbed under great duress, a pass we could intercept.

Diagram 8-7 displays a drill we use to teach coverage of the middle and the backdoor cutters. We combine both cuts into one drill.

Procedure (Diagram 8-7):

1. Line up four offensive players and four defensive players. After you are satisfied with your defense, rotate from offense to defense and defense to offense.
2. 1 passes to 2 and cuts on a middle cut or a backdoor cut. 4, if it is a middle cut as the diagram shows, rotates down to a guard and 1 becomes an offensive forward.

3. X1 and X4 must cover the cutter according to rule number 3.

4. 2 then passes to 4 and cuts backdoor or middle. 3 replaces 2. X2 and X3 operate under rule number 3.

5. We begin by limiting the cuts to one or the other—middle or backdoor. Once we are pleased with the defense, we allow the offense to decide its cut.

6. The goalie can be drilled on coverage of the lob pass.

Objectives:

1. To teach defenders to cover middle and backdoor cutters.

2. To teach defenders how to cover downfloor when passes are made from one lane to another.

3. To teach proper defensive rotation.

4. Defensive coverage off of the ball. The front line defender should never get farther away than 10 from the ball (40 into 30, for example). The back line defender may get as far away as 30 from the ball, but he should not consider more than 20 away, even less when there is a cutter from behind the back line defense. These definitions of area coverage correspond to the principles described in Chapter 5 (Keep Proper Spacing).

Diagram 8-8 exemplifies excellent coverage. X1 defends 1 tightly, trying to get him to dribble and keeping him from immediately spotting 3's flash pivot maneuver. X3 plays where he can see the ball and any cutter coming into the middle lane. He must prevent the flash pivot. X4 plays denial, but with a proper float on the next vertical pass in the ball lane. X5 plays for the lob pass to X4's man, to X3's man, or to the off-ball lane. Any pass from 1 over the head of X3 or X4 could bring an immediate two-man jump between X5 and the defender on the intended receiver (same as in Diagram 8-3).

It would be futile to imply that the offense will never complete a pass into the middle lane. When they do complete such a pass, we rotate in the manner shown in Diagram 8-9. X3 takes 3, X1 and X2 rotate to the wings, and X4 takes short safety. When the ball is in the middle lane, we give the 1-2-1-1 zone press look. When the ball is in the outside lanes, we show the 2-2-1 line up. X5 still plays goalie.

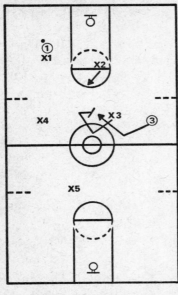

Diagram 8-8

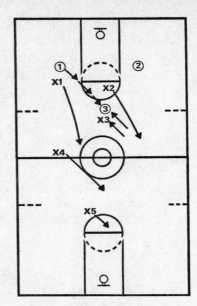

Diagram 8-9

5. Defensive rotations out of unsuccessful traps. When the double-teamed attacker successfully completes a pass out of the trap, the container rotates to the next open man or area while the trapper takes the double-teamed passer. This is the same rule we use in all our stunts. Consistency in the rules makes for easier learning and more efficient execution.

6. Coverage when ball is in the middle lane. When an attacker has the ball in the middle lane, we want a 1-2-1-1 alignment. We want the defender on the ball to play his man aggressively, trying to force him to begin his dribble out of the middle lane. We want the wings to sink toward the ball but still maintain good man-to-man coverage on the men in their areas.

To advance the ball up the floor, this middle attacker must dribble or pass. When the ball is dribbled from the middle lane, we want the wing defender in the direction that the ball is being dribbled to activate a two-man jump with the dribbler's defender. We call this automatically, unless we have a stunt called from the ball lane (such as, give the outside and then take it away). If such a stunt has been called, we expect the middle lane defender to force the dribbler toward the sideline before impelling him to reverse dribble back toward the middle. As the reverse dribble begins, the defenders commence their stunt. We have two options available: We can two-man jump prior to giving the outside and then taking it away, or we can let the middle defender keep the dribbler and let him give the outside then take it away.

When the ball is passed out of the middle lane toward a side lane, the rotation would again give the appearance of a 2-2-1 zone press. Diagram 8-10 illustrates the correct coverage. X1 would become the front defender in the ball lane, X2 the front middle defender, X3 the deep middle defender, and X4 the deep ball lane defender. X5 is still the goalie.

Diagram 8-9 also provides an opportunity to discuss a pass from a side lane into the middle lane. This should only happen on non-penetrating passes (Diagram 8-9 shows a penetrating pass). If 1 had passed to 2, the middle lane front defender would have taken the receiver, 2. X1 would become a wing along with the deep middle defender, X3. The deep ball side defender, X4, would become the short safety. If 1 cuts middle or backdoor, X1 would activate rule number 3 with X4.

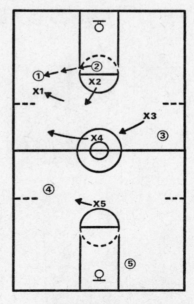

Diagram 8-10

7. *Middle deep defender stops the breakaway dribbler.*
This axiom demands the same rotation as the principle in Chapter 5: Weakside defender stops the breakaway dribbler. Because the postulates of the run and jump, the area man-to-man, and the basic man are all consistent, it becomes easier to teach the players and simpler for them to learn and apply the presses. But the subtle differences in the three make it difficult for offensive teams to successfully attack them.

In Diagram 8-11, 1 drives by X1. X2 could not close the gap, making 1 a breakaway dribbler. It becomes X3's responsibility to stop 1. X1 stays with 1 until X3 yells "jump." X3 now becomes a front defender. X2 becomes a deep defender (a wing if 1 is in the center lane). X4 plays denial and stays as a deep defender. X1 is either a wing or a front defender, depending on where 1 dribbles the ball. X1 is a wing if the ball is in the middle lane.

Diagram 8-12 shows 1 driving around X1 to the outside. Defenders use the same coverage. X2 and X3, for example, exchange front and deep coverage. X4 still covers deep, and X1

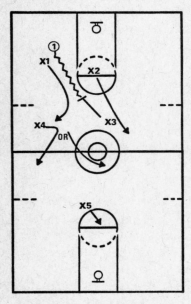

Diagram 8-11

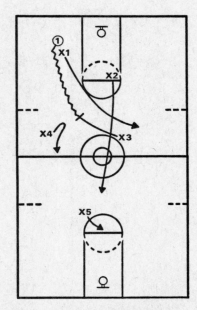

Diagram 8-12

rotates to the open front spot (which is the side he was covering 1 on). When 1 drives by X1, X4 hedges, but is too far away to close the gap for X1. X3 must stop the breakaway dribbler. X2 rotates to deep coverage. If the ball is in the middle lane, X1 and X4 would be wings and X2 would be the short safety.

When a dribbler breaks by the front line, the defender responsible for stopping the dribbler must exercise caution. He must control and slow down the dribbler before trying to channel him. He can do this by dropping and delaying, dropping and delaying. Otherwise, the dribbler would break free and a fast-break lay-up would result.

Diagrams 8-5 through 8-12 can be used as individual drills; or the coach can combine them into a single four-on-four team drill. We drill both ways. But when we work on the four-on-four shell drill, we always emphasize at least one individual point before allowing the players to free-lance. For instance, we might require a flash pivot pass completion, a breakaway dribbler stopped, or a few backdoor or middle cuts before permitting free-lance cuts.

8. The goalie's coverage. The goalie must watch the ball handler. He must read and anticipate the intentions of this potential passer. The goalie has no responsibilities toward the dribbler. he can concentrate on the long lob pass.

If a team attacks with five players in the back court, the goalie moves into back court and plays the man in the middle lane man-to-man. The goalie would become one of the four perimeter defenders if a perimeter deep attacker takes his man deep. The perimeter deep attacker's defender stays with the cutter going deep, becoming the new goalie. In other words, the goalie and perimeter deep defender exchange responsibilities.

If a team attacks by throwing the lob pass to the off-ball lane, the goalie should place one foot in the center lane and one foot in the off-ball lane and locate at the end of area 10 (if the ball is in area 40). This gives him perfect positioning to intercept this pass.

If a team attacks by a lob pass into the center lane or into the ball lane, the goalie should place one foot in the ball lane and one foot in the center lane and situate at the end of area 10 (if the ball is in area 40). This provides him with a good interception angle.

When the ball handler begins his dribble, the goalie can cheat up to the beginning of area 10 (midcourt). From there he can enter into one of the stunts if he feels he has a good interception opportunity (if a 5 is called he must enter the stunt).

However, we want him to always consider defense of the basket area as his first responsibility. Because his first duty is to prevent the lay-up, the goalie would vacate the basket area only when he sees that a teammate can cover for him. He must master the drill dealing with this coverage in Chapter 6.

The goalie has full view of the action. He can help his teammates by telling them where the offense intends to attack.

Summary of the rules. These rules are designed to force the lob pass, eliminate the clearout, eradicate the short passing game, and stifle any dribble with stunts. These rules even provide an adequate defense should there be a breakdown of the primary defensive coverage. Face-guarding, short-stopping, left field, and center field techniques offer available in-bound coverage, and we try to intercept all in-bound passes or force a five-second violation. If the offensive team passes that first test, they must still pass or dribble through the web woven by the area man-to-man press. And we hope our rules will make it impossible for the dribbling fly to escape the defensive spider's web, either by passing or by dribbling. If they should escape, we have pre-planned adjustments to tighten the web (see the Forty, Thirty, Twenty, and Ten Series).

PLACEMENT OF PERSONNEL

All players should know the duties and responsibilities of each area. They may have to play all areas during any game. Their positioning depends a great deal upon the location of their men. What the attackers attempt to accomplish and how they intend to achieve that goal will make a difference. What we want to force the offense to do is another consideration.

Some offenses only want to get the ball over the time line. Such attacks can be unmercifully pressed, without fear of giving an easy uncontested shot. Others try to pressure the defense by relentlessly attacking the basket. These teams must be defensed from basket to basket. Still others operate between the extremes. When we face the non-basket attacking teams, we place our quicker and more gambling players up front. When we play the fast breaking teams, we place our quicker player in the back line and a taller player as a goalie.

Some teams use only a passing attack. They may use the short passing game or the long lob game. In either case, we use our taller and slower personnel up front. This prevents the passer from having an unencumbered view. It also encourages the passer to become a dribbler, and a dribbler is the fly headed into our defensive web (see sections on Forty, Thirty, Twenty, and Ten Series). This passer usually feels he is quicker and can beat his taller and slower defender on the dribble. And no team has ever beaten the area press with a dribble attack. Occasionally, a dribbler will break away, but he will not escape enough times via the dribbler's route to damage the team that presses 60 possessions or more a game.

When you play the team that tries to dribble through the press, it does not matter where you place your personnel. If you intend to trap or jump, placing the bigger and slower players up front will work best. If you intend to contain and delay, the slower players should be placed on the back line and at the goal line.

If a team passes off the dribble as they see a trap or a jump approaching, that team should face the bigger, slower defenders up front. That enables the quicker players to shoot the gap from the back line where they can see and react as the slower players signal their intentions.

GIVING THE ZONE LOOK

If we have no defender on the out-of-bounds passer, the defense will look like a 2-2-1 zone press with each defender defensing the first man in his area. If there is a defender on the out-of-bounds passer, the defense appears to be a 1-2-1-1 zone press. Of course, we could be in one of these zones; or we could be in a man press, picking up the first man in our area and playing run and jump into front court. Or, we could be in the area man-to-man press.

If we are in our area man-to-man press, we can still go zone after the in-bounds pass, we can go straight man, or we can go area man, running the forty, thirty, twenty, or ten series. We can keep the offense guessing. We can keep them off-balance and confused.

Show zone go man. When we show zone go man, it is usually against teams that like to advance with a passing attack. If we keep each potential receiver covered, the passer must become a dribbler. We can run and jump this dribbler, forcing the pass off of the dribble.

Show man go man. We use this strategy to keep pressure on the offense. This is used mainly in the last part of the second quarter and the early part of the third. It keeps pressure on the attackers, and it helps us determine what stunts we want to activate in the second half. It also gives the other coach something to waste time on by discussing it during the half-time break.

Show zone go zone. This strategy is valuable against poor passing teams and teams that move away from the ball poorly. It is also a good strategy after a team has abandoned their team attack. The area man-to-man press will impel teams to discard their team strategy (see the sections on the Forty, Thirty, Twenty, and Ten Series). We also like to show zone go zone when a team is hurting our man press with an attack we have not drilled against. For example, a team may have us outmanned at several positions, thereby creating some breakaway opportunities. We show zone go zone until we can work out a better placement of personnel. Then we go back to the area press which is strong against the pass and devastating against the dribble.

Show man go zone. We use this to try to steal or deflect the in-bounds pass or to create the five-second turnover; and also when we want to immediately double-team upon the in-bounds completion. Of course, we still have the blitz trap which would represent a show man go man.

The defensive coach can choose among the strategies above, the tactics of the two- and three-man stunts, or the devices of the area man-to-man press. He can even wait until after the first pass to switch from zone to man or from man to zone. Or he can call several individual, two-man, or three-man stunts in succession (see Chapter 6). They all work to confuse the attackers. They all work together to make the area man-to-man impregnable.

ROTATING FROM A 2-2-1 TO A 1-2-1-1 LOOK

By activating rule number 1 of the area man-to-man press, the coach will switch his defense from a 2-2-1 look to a 1-2-1-1 look. Anytime a ball is passed from an outside lane to the middle lane, the defense shifts from a 2-2-1 alignment to a 1-2-1-1 array. If the coach chooses to trap the initial in-bounds pass, he has a 1-2-1-1 coverage.

ROTATING FROM A 1-2-1-1 TO A 2-2-1 LOOK

If the defense does not trap on the in-bounds pass, the defender on the out-of-bounds passer drops toward the free throw line. This creates the impression of going from 1-2-1-1 to a 2-2-1 zone press. A pass from the middle lane, where the press looks like a 1-2-1-1 zone press, to an outside lane would change the zone from a 1-2-1-1 to a 2-2-1 look. A dribble from the middle lane to an outside lane would present the same effect.

Both of the last two sections could actually be zone presses if the coach is in a show zone go zone strategy. But if the coach has activated the area man-to-man press, these are only zone looks. The defense is actually man-to-man using a few zone principles.

THE FORTY SERIES

Diagram 8-4 divides the full court pressing areas into four sections: 40, 30, 20, and 10. These sections tell defenders where we want a trap, a jump, or a stunt to occur. The second number relates how many defenders are involved. So 32 indicates two defenders trapping or jumping in the area between the free throw line and the 28-foot marker. 43 means a trap or jump by three defenders in the area between the end line and the free throw line. "43 faceguard" would be the same trap or jump, only the in-bounds attackers would be denied the ball. 143 places a defender on the out-of-bounds passer. Two digits represent showing zone going man. Three-digit numbers above 200 indicate zone or man coverage. 243 means show zone go zone. 343 tells our defenders to show man go zone. 443 tells the defenders to show man go man.

Because 42, 32, 22, and 12 represent the same coverage, just at different spots on the floor, we will explain only one series in detail. We will illustrate and explain the thirty series and why and when we use the other series.

Immediate pressure can be placed on the attacking team in a forty series. Recovery time is greatest from the forty area should the defense make a mistake. And, we begin our alignment of defenders in the forty area even if 12 is called. This way we keep the attackers guessing as we retreat with the advancing ball to the 10 area. Dribblers, under such conditions, never know when to pass and when to dribble. They never know when we will retreat without a challenge. They never know when the traps or jumps will occur. Defenders know; and because of that knowledge, they can cheat steps to achieve better interception angles.

Although we try to be versatile in our calls, the forty series is run more frequently against weak or inexperienced guards. The forty series becomes a bread-and-butter maneuver in periods of great momentum or when the opposition abandons their planned attack, thereby becoming unpoised. And the forty series is available as a change of pace when another series might be more advantageous.

THE THIRTY SERIES

When we allow the in-bounds pass, we frequently run the thirty series. It is the second best area from defensive recovery time. When teams do not pass well off of the dribble, we enlist the thirty series. We allow the in-bounds pass. We force the dribble by covering all potential pass receivers and by putting immense pressure on the ball handler. Then we spring the trap or the jump. The thirty series also works well against the team that likes to attack with the short passing game or the team that prefers the dribble-pass—dribble-pass method of advancing the ball.

32. We do not care which direction the ball handler drives. We allow the ball handler to choose. Or the coach could call "fan" or "funnel," giving the off-ball defenders another opportunity to cheat a few steps toward the interception lanes.

Diagram 8-13 shows 1, the dribbler, driving to the outside. X1 stays in control coverage of 1 until X4 yells "trap" or "jump." A jump would have X1 and X4 rotating positions. A trap would have X1 and X4 double-teaming 1 while X2, X3, and X5 would play their men (show zone go man or show man go man) or the passing lanes (show zone go zone or show man go zone).

Let's assume that we are playing man in all the illustrations, but the reader should remain aware that we can go zone. By assuming only man coverage, we can illustrate the amazing adjustability of the area man-to-man press. But if the coach wishes to go zone, X2, X3, and X5 must read the passing lanes and get in them (see Chapter 2). Also, let's assume X5 is quick enough to cover a passing lane if you go man or go zone. If X5 is not quick enough, he can play goalie exclusively. Naturally, however, a press is better if all five defenders can press.

1 would make the obvious pass if X1 and X4 trap and the other defenders are in man coverage. 1 would probably make

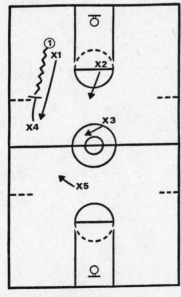

Diagram 8-13

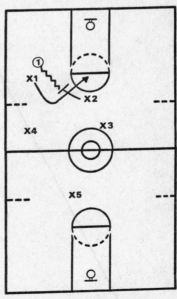

Diagram 8-14

the same pass if X4 yelled "jump." After an obvious pass or two, 33, 34, or 35 would close that obvious passing lane, often resulting in a steal.

Diagram 8-14 illustrates 32 with 1 driving to the middle. The obvious pass is no threat (a horizontal pass). X1 and X2 run and jump trap or switch. X3 and X4 play their positions according to 1's position on the floor. If 1 is located in an outside lane, X3 and X4 defend the middle and the ball lane. If 1 has dribbled into the middle lane, X1 and X4 are wing defenders and X3 covers the middle lane in a 1-2-1-1 look.

A drive by 1 toward the middle lane should be met with "trap" more often than "jump." X1 could still recover if 1 should complete the obvious pass out of the trap. Any deflection would result in an easy basket. The downcourt passing lanes are easily covered. And 33, 34, or 35 frequently force a turnover.

33. Diagram 8-15 represents accurate coverage when 1 drives outside and 33 is called. X4 yells "jump" or "trap." If 32 has been run a few times and if 1 has been making the obvious pass, X3 will intercept. X3 becomes a gap shooter, leaving his man when X4 leaves. X1 rotates to X3's vacated area.

Diagram 8-16 depicts the inside drive. X2 calls "jump" or "trap." X3 again becomes the gap shooter. An easy point for defenders to remember: The deep defender away from the dribbler always becomes the gap shooter. X1 rotates to the area vacated by X3.

In both of these diagrams, the open area for an immediate pass off of the dribble is to the region just vacated by X3. 32, 34, or 35 would, however, close that area. 1 is not sure of the defensive call, and any momentary hesitation on 1's part would result in X1 closing the open area. 1 will most likely pick up his dribble because he is not sure if it is a trap or a jump. If 1 does pick up his dribble, the other four defenders would hear "used" from the trapper. This tells the off of the ball defenders to deny any man in their area any pass.

34. Diagram 8-17 shows 1 on the outside drive against a 34 call. X4 is the trapper with the responsibility of calling "trap" or "jump." X4 would also call "used" if 1 picks up his dribble. X3 closes the obvious passing lane. X2 seals off the lane that was open in the 33 calls. X1 rotates to the up position in the middle lane.

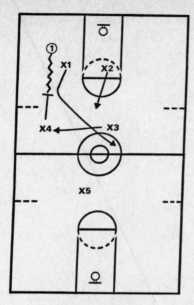

Diagram 8-15

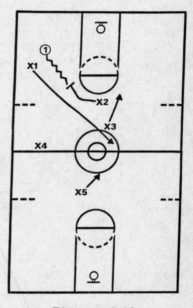

Diagram 8-16

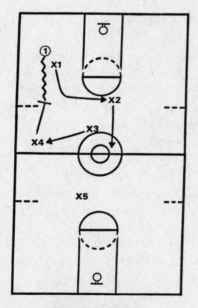

Diagram 8-17

Diagram 8-18 relates the defensive coverage on the middle drive by 1. X3 shoots the gap on the obvious passing lane. X4 covers the lane that was open during the 33 calls. X1, the container, rotates to the open area or the open man.

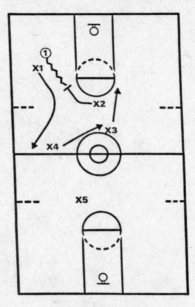

Diagram 8-18

35. We seldom activate the goalie unless it is late and we need to steal a pass or unless we intend to show man go zone. 35 rotates into perfect zone coverage. X4 stops the dribble, yelling "jump" or "trap" (Diagram 8-19). X5 takes X4's man. X3 rotates deep for the lob pass coverage, becoming the goalie. X2 covers the area vacated by X3. And X1, the container, rotates to the open area or the open man.

Diagram 8-20 depicts the coverage on the inside drive. X2, the trapper, stops 1; X3 "gap shoots" the obvious passing lane; X5 covers the area vacated by X3; and X4 rotates to goalie coverage.

If we are in a trap coverage with intentions of going zone, X4 would pause to cover the ball lane before rotating to deep coverage. X5 must choose his coverage under zone conditions.

X5's first thought must be coverage of the basket area. His second concern is the area vacated by X3.

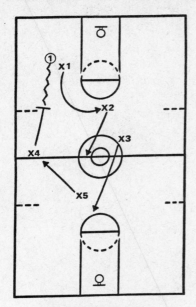

Diagram 8-19

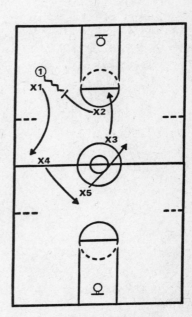

Diagram 8-20

X5 has many advantages. He should know 1's passing pattern, especially if 32, 33, and 34 have been run. X5 also knows that 1 has been trapped and it is difficult for him to find a deep receiver under trapping conditions from the 30 area.

As the reader can see, the area man-to-man press adjusts to cover the open passing lanes: What was open under 32 is closed by 33, 34, and 35. Dribblers must find the open lane: They only have a moment to find it. And if they guess wrong while passing off of the dribble, the pass will be intercepted. If the dribbler picks up his dribble to look cautiously for a receiver, the defenders will have enough recovery time to cover all potential receivers (the dribble "used" drill). If the dribbler tries to keep his dribble alive, the trapper merely calls "trap" before he yells "used."

The web begins to strangle the fly. The spider approaches. The fly gets nervous, losing his poise. Chaotic conditions set in. Before long, the fly succumbs.

Coaches can add the stunts of Chapters 2, 3, and 4 by assigning those stunts numbers. Let's assign the number 6 to the give-the-outside-then-take-it-away stunt. 36, therefore, would define the give-the-outside-then-take-it-away stunt occurring in area 30. Diagram 8-21 shows the typical coverage.

1 is given the outside by X1. X1 stops 1 in the 30 area. 1 reverse dribbles only to find X2 trapping or jumping. X3 has the option of shooting the gap (or the coach can call a 6 stunt under 33—three-man rotation out of the give-the-outside-then-take-it-away stunt). X4 can be involved in the rotation, as can X5. Or the coach can use the stunt to go zone.

THE TWENTY SERIES

Traps and jumps that occur just before the time line can compel the dribbler to worry about a ten-second violation. When we run the twenties, we begin in a 2-2-1 alignment in area 40 and drop slowly as the dribbler advances the ball. After we have delayed the dribbler a few seconds, the ball will approach the midcourt line. A trap or a jump may panic an unpoised dribbler, especially if he has already faced the forty or thirty series.

THE TEN SERIES

The ten series works best against the smooth-functioning patterned teams. These teams have been taught to get a good shot off of their patterns by running and rerunning their options until the good shot develops. The ten series can force these teams into errors with little chance of conceding a basket. If the team quickly attacks the open lane, they would leave their patterned attack. They have been conditioned not to do that. Even a score under such conditions works in favor of the defense: It can get the offense to rushing and out of their methodical attack.

Patterned teams are usually well-oiled, beautifully poised,

slow-moving machines. Such teams would keep their patience until they weaved their way through the area web, slowing down the pace of the game. But hitting them with the ten series could force them out of their patterned attack into a quicker tempo.

When we run the ten series, we can still begin our press in area 40. We repeatedly drop and delay as the ball advances. When the ball reaches area 10, we trap or jump. Of course, we can, as an option, start the press from areas 10, 20, or 30.

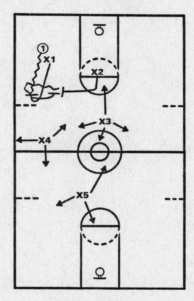

Diagram 8-21

9

Defensing the Best Known Methods of Attacking the Man Press

There are as many types of press offenses as there are coaches, but all full court attacks incorporate certain basic elements. Being aware of these and working daily on defensing them helps the defense recognize reoccurring situations during ball games. This chapter shows how to defense these popular principles of assault. We do not attempt to explain all the techniques a defensive coach can employ. We offer some suggestions, leaving it to you to decide which you prefer.

FLASHING AND POSTING

Some coaches, regardless of their initial alignment, choose to have a player break into the middle lane for a pass. If the pass does not occur momentarily, this flash pivot attacker begins to post, trying to get the defender on his back, waiting for the penetrating pass. Any time the pass comes to this player, he immediately pivots to check downcourt for another poster in the middle lane, or he looks to the opposite side lane from whence the ball entered.

To defense this method of attack, we exaggerate a slough into the middle lane. Not only does this give us good positioning to deny the flash pivot the ball on his initial cut, but it frequently forces the lob pass into the off-ball lane. This is a difficult pass for the offense to complete and an easy one for the defense to intercept.

When the attacker tries to post, our defender gets several feet off of him in the line between the ball and the poster. The defender places his ear on the poster's chest, only about three or four feet away. He puts an arm, a leg, and his head in that passing lane. He must see both the poster and the ball.

We do not fear the lob; we must prevent the direct pass to the middle lane. A lob pass brings the offense out of their intended method of attack. A lob often results in a deflection, an interception, or a charge.

If we are in a run and jump and the opposition employs a stationary post, we would not put the poster's defender in the jump rotation. But if this poster was an obvious pass receiver and was definitely the passer's first preference, we might place this defender in the rotation and try to shoot the gap for some steals.

Your defense must also consider your personnel and your opponents. But the defensive coach must have worked on methods of keeping the ball out of the middle lane, to either a flash pivot attacker or a player who posts, if his press is to be successful.

SIDELINE TYPE OFFENSES

Some offensive-minded coaches believe it best to break a press by passing down the sidelines. They reason that deflections would go out-of-bounds, that interceptions would be fewer because the interceptor would probably touch the sideline as he intercepted the ball, and that completions would break the press.

Throughout this book you have noticed that we deflect toward the middle lane all passes directed down the sidelines. We drill and drill and drill on this. And we always have a defender assigned to the recovery area in the middle lane.

We grant that it is more difficult for a moving defender to intercept a pass in the outside lanes because his momentum will frequently carry him out-of-bounds. We want these defenders to arrive early and to become stationary moments before the interception. If an interception is not possible, we want the defender to deflect the ball toward the middle, not out-of-bounds.

Denial defense of the attacker in the ball lane prevents passes from being thrown directly into the outside ball lane. A cross-court pass would have to be attempted to get the ball to the opposite outside lane. Denial ball lane defense can be played using our stunts, our run and jump press, or our area man-to-man press. All three help check and defeat the sideline type offenses.

MIDDLE LANE OFFENSES

Coaches who prefer to attack the middle lane reason they have more passing avenues available from the middle. They reason that all those passing lanes from the middle cannot be covered with only five defenders. They tell their players to post or flash into the middle lane, receive the ball, check downcourt in the middle lane, then check the outside lane opposite the entry pass.

Sagging the off-ball defenders clogs the middle. By using our floating rule of playing two-thirds the distance from the ball and one-third the distance from our man, we can prevent the flash pivot. If teams have trouble getting the ball into the middle lane, they look elsewhere to advance the ball.

Constant drilling on the proper techniques will reduce the threat of the penetrating pass to the middle lane. If the offense is unable to pass into the middle, they quickly abandon this attack. Interceptions on forced passes into the middle usually result in a lay-up. A few interceptions quickly deter the middle lane attack. Tremendous pressure on the ball handler aids in these interceptions.

Team techniques can be employed to close the road down the middle. Where funnelling techniques would close the sideline attack, fanning methods would deny the middle route. Giving the outside and then taking it away encourages the outside dribble. The quick trap on the reverse dribble presents the ball handler a poor passing avenue into the middle lane and awards the defender on the flash pivot attacker a perfect interception angle. Both the run and jump press (Chapter 7) and the area man-to-man press (Chapter 8) can concentrate on defeating the middle lane attack.

SHORT PASS GAME

Many coaches believe that the best offense against a press is the short passing attack. They may want to go down the sideline, down the middle, or a combination of the two. Teams that advance the ball with a series of short passes must be defensed in a manner that encourages the dribble or the long pass. This takes them out of their game and into the jaws of the defense.

The area man-to-man press discourages the short pass and induces the dribble and the long pass. By playing denial defense on potential receivers one man removed from the ball, we discourage the short pass. By leaving the off-ball lane open, teams look to lob a long pass into that area. As you know from Chapter 8, we hope for this pass. We drill on anticipating it and on intercepting it. We pressure the ball handler, trying to keep him from finding the open man, trying to compel the dribble. Then we have stunts to destroy the dribble.

The run and jump press leads to many interceptions of the short passing game. By pressuring the ball handler into a dribble and by the trapper's proper approach to that dribbler, we encourage the quick obvious pass off of the dribble. This short pass can be stolen by an alert gap shooter.

All the two- and three-man stunts of Chapters 2, 3, 4, and 6 are designed to eliminate the short passes. Defensive coaches can study the favorite methods of the attacking passer and engage the stunt that best defeats those methods. For example, does the passer pass off of the dribble (run and jump or area press), does he bend around a trapper for the slow bounce pass (trapping with a gap shooter)? Most passers alternate their methods, but all have a favorite one. It is up to you to determine what that favorite method is in order to defense it.

LONG PASS GAME

Research indicates that over half of the baseball passes thrown result in turnovers. Either the pass itself is thrown away, it is intercepted, or the intended receiver overextends himself, committing a violation (especially charging or walking). The two-handed overhead pass produces a somewhat better statistical result. More concentrated practice on the baseball and two-handed overhead passes could raise the percentage. But even then, at the high school level, the efficiency of the long pass game could never equal the other offensive options. This knowledge leads many coaches to describe the long pass game as "cow pasture basketball."

Our defenses are designed to compel the long pass game; consequently, our players are more than adequately drilled on defending it. Pressure on the passer and individual coverage downcourt conquers the long pass, but it does not encourage it. We run our area man-to-man press to induce the long pass. We run our left field when we are sure that teams will run a long pass pattern, such as the Virginia Box (see later section in this chapter).

Long pass teams will commit enough errors to give you the game even if you have not drilled on proper coverage. Any stunt that keeps adequate downfloor coverage with proper sags can force the violation, intercept the pass, or impel the passer to push the ball too far and out-of-bounds.

DRIBBLE AND SPLIT GAME

Some coaches like to dribble against full court pressure. And when a double-team approaches their talented and experienced dribbler, they have the dribbler-penetrator split the two defenders. The split can occur in two ways: The dribbler can fake dribbling one way before driving between the defenders; or the dribbler can leap into the air between the potential double-teamers, passing the ball to a teammate before he lands.

A team would need a talented dribbler-passer to achieve success with this method. So most coaches work diligently to develop great dribbler-passers. Most boys begin in the Junior Pro program developing their ball-handling skills.

It used to be taboo to pass crosscourt against a zone. Today it has become an accepted mode of attack, and a rather successful one. Down through the years, coaches have forbidden their players to leave the floor to pass the ball. But with the emergence of modern ball-handling skills, this method of penetration has become standard.

How do you stop the dribble and split game? First, you work extremely hard on your double-teaming techniques (see Chapter 2). If the driver-passer is so skilled that he breaks tight double-teams consistently, then the coach must employ the loose double-team. This should contain the skilled penetrator, and it should get the trap set. Any coverage of the passing lanes that is successful can be instituted (zone, straight man, run and jump, etc.). We like to run the area man-to-man press against this skilled dribbler.

Two- and three-man stunts are effective against this attacker. Because his coach has designated him as the ball handler, he expects to handle the ball. Short-stopping can prevent him from getting the in-bounds pass. A run and jump trap can compel him to give up the ball if he gets away from the short stop. Face-guarding him after he gives it up can postpone his

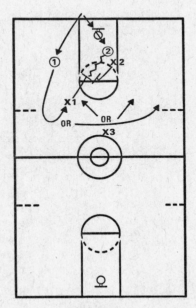

Diagram 9-1

receiving it back. If you have one great defender who can neutralize the expert penetrator, the run and no-jump philosophy will work best.

"78" has given us our best stunt coverage. Diagram 9-1 depicts a typical show-and-tell coverage (see Chapter 6). X2 plays the expert dribbler, and X1 follows the clearout in-bounds passer. X1 stops about 20 feet away, intending to trap with X2. 1 becomes the obvious pass receiver. 1 can stay in his clearout lane or he can loop to the lane 2 leaves. X3 plays 1 at a profitable interception angle. As 2 leaps into the air to split the double-team, X3 leaves to intercept the pass to 1. You can activate X4 to shoot the gap on the attacker X3 left. This is especially advisable after X3 makes a few interceptions.

PATTERNED OFFENSES

Patterned offenses offer the poorest choice to the offensive coach. Two or three patterns are easily scouted, easily defended. After a few runnings in the first quarter, the defense adjusts and the patterns become totally ineffective. A larger number of patterns would make the attack too complicated, too hard for the players to learn much less execute. Yet many basketball coaches continue to teach patterns. And they continue to wonder why their offenses are unsuccessful.

We open nearly every game with our three-men-and-a-tandem (or a gap) stunt against teams we have not scouted. We try to make this stunt look like a zone press. Our opposition usually responds with their practiced patterned team offense. We assign one assistant coach to diagram these patterns for us. After three or four first-quarter possessions, we know the offense we will face for that night. We judge which stunt or team press we think will be most effective. We experiment until early in the second quarter. Then we run straight man-to-man or some stunts until the third quarter, when we activate the most effective press. Our team becomes acquainted with their offense at the time-outs and during half-time.

Teams cannot learn enough patterns to be effective at both the full court and the half-court level. They cannot be confidentially prepared pattern-wise for both. But they must be if they intend to defeat the man-to-man full court and the man-to-man half-court.

THE VIRGINIA BOX

A good example of a patterned attack is the Virginia Box. It puts five attackers in back court. It is designed to get the long pass entry or to get the in-bounds pass against denial pressure.

Teams using the Virginia Box to overcome denial in-bounds pressure will be met by a left fielder (Diagram 9-2). Also, the Virginia Box permits a long in-bounds pass to either 4 or 5 on the fly route. The defender on 1, X1, becomes the left fielder, positioning himself at the defensive free throw line. The left fielder would intercept any long pass. He could draw the charge off any deep cutter.

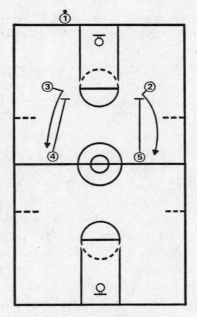

Diagram 9-2

4 and 5 screen down on X2 and X3. 2 and 3 run the deep fly route while 4 and 5 criss-cross, screen for each other, or break to the ball to get open. Once the ball is in-bounded, either 3 or 2

(or both) break back to half-court for a release pass. 3 or 2 can break back in an outside lane or they can use the middle lane. They can post or flash pivot. They can come all the way back for a short passing game, or they can stay in front court for the long pass.

Coaches who do not wish to take the pressure off of the out-of-bounds passer can activate the area man-to-man press. By proper rotation, the defense would still have a deep safety to intercept the long pass. The defense would also have pressure on the passer, hampering his view, forcing a higher pass, eliminating the baseball pass.

If a coach suspects his next opponent will use the Virginia Box, he can drill on the fundamentals of defensing the inbounding of the ball to vertical and deep cutters, and of defensing the screening maneuvers of Chapter 3. He can add to this coverage several team techniques once the ball has been inbounded: the run and jump, the area press, or two- or three-man stunts. Again, evaluation of defensive personnel and the opponent's players will help the coach make his decision.

THE ONE-MAN ATTACK: THE CLEAROUT

Most coaches attack straight man-to-man defensive pressure with one man dribbling while the other attackers clear out. The dribbler, after receiving the in-bounds pass, usually waits until his teammates are gone before he begins his dribble.

Teams that clear out operate under a negative attack approach. They simply want to get the ball into front court and begin their half-court patterned offense.

All the stunts of this book work against teams who clear out. And the defenders can gamble more. Defenders know the defensive goal is well protected; they also know that the clearout teams are usually negative.

The area man-to-man ten series causes clearout players trouble. The area can be run from 40 back into 10 or by starting the defenders in area 10.

Against clearout teams, the defense can fight the advancement of the ball every inch of the floor. Two or three successive stunts can be employed.

Zone presses would eliminate the clearout, giving defensive

teams two options. They can employ the zone press to eliminate the clearout when it is hurting them. But, mostly, they should like to face the clearout. They should occasionally employ the area press (showing zone some) to keep the attackers off-balance.

Clearouts should offer few or no problems. These teams should experience extreme difficulty in getting the ball inbounds, in advancing it up the floor, in setting up their half-court offense. In short, they should be pressed unmercifully.

THE 2 DOWN-3 BACK ATTACK

Not only do we categorize our opponent's attack by method, but we also classify their assault by the number participating. 2 down-3 back indicates that our opponents intend to break our full court defense with two clever ball handlers. Their offense will show three men in the front court.

When this alignment is used as a team attack, it indicates that a coach has two expert ball handlers. This array will be used more when a team is facing man-to-man full court pressure. It will be used less against zone pressure.

Teams will run the 2 down-3 back formation against our stunts and our team run and jump (Chapter 7). But these teams will probably bring more attackers downfloor to face the area man-to-man or the zone presses.

When teams use only two players to attack our area press, we might run the area press the entire night. Or we might run the area press just to force our opposition to bring more attackers into back court.

We often meet the 2 down-3 back attack with a three-man and a gap stunt. This gives us a chance to run and jump and shoot the gap without giving the lay-up at our defensive end.

Diagram 9-3 displays a stunt we use against both the clearout and the 2 down-3 back assaults. X1 guides 1 down the sideline into front court. As 1 nears front court, X4 races hard to activate the long run and jump trap. X4 plans his move so that he can trap 1 just as he crosses the midcourt line. X5 shoots the gap on the lane to 4. X3 covers 5, and X2 zones between 2 and 3. If 1 picks up his dribble, X4 can yell "used." If "used" becomes operative, X2 would cover 3 and X1 would cover 2. After five seconds elapse, a jump ball will result. To help this stunt, the defensive coach could scout his opponent. Once the half-court formation is known, he can pass the information to his players, making it easier to cover the passing lanes.

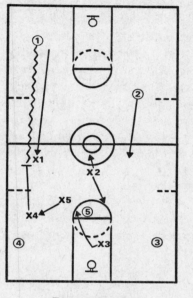

Diagram 9-3

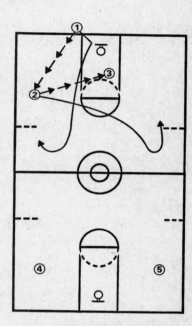

Diagram 9-4

THE 3 DOWN-2 BACK ATTACK

Teams that use three players to bring the ball up the floor usually have drilled movements which border on three-man patterned play. They can use cuts or screens or both.

Diagram 9-4 represents a three-man cutting movement. 1 passes to 2 and tries a middle cut. After reaching midcourt, 1 either posts in the middle lane or breaks back toward the ball in the ball lane. Meanwhile, 3 has broken to an open spot. 2 could dribble up the court as far as the defense would allow before passing to 3. 2 immediately middle cuts. 2, after going 30 or so feet downfloor, would post in the middle lane or would buttonhook back toward the ball in the ball lane. Meanwhile, 1 would be hunting daylight while 3 penetrates with a dribble as far as the defense will permit. And the process continues.

The offense can use this crossing pattern in a dribble and split game, as a sideline offense, or as a middle posting offense. Any quick pass to the middle cutter would result in a three lane fast-break. Of course, 4 and/or 5 could break back to midcourt as a safety valve. But that would represent the 5-down attack.

Left-fielding, center-fielding, short-stopping, face-guarding, and denial offer possible in-bounds coverage. After the opposition successfully in-bounds the ball, it is best to activate a team stunt or press. Three-on-three run and jump coverage usually slows down the offense, but it will not conquer the widely-spread offensive movement. Fanning techniques can help the team stunts of Chapter 6 or the team presses of Chapters 7 and 8.

Immediate and constant pressure must be kept on the dribbler-penetrator. We want to encourage the dribble rather than let the attackers pick us to death with accurate passes to the middle cutters. The blitz trap on the in-bounds pass can force a turnover or two.

THE 4 DOWN-1 BACK ATTACK

The 4 down-1 back attack borders on a patterned scheme. In fact, many teams like to leave a player near the basket in their patterned movements against full court pressure.

Four or more attackers in back court play into the hands of our stunts. Any stunt in this book should prove successful. Our team stunts (Chapter 6) or our team presses (Chapters 7 and 8) should destroy four attackers congregated in the small area of the back court.

THE 5 DOWN-0 BACK ATTACK

This attack is usually completely patterned. Some teams will only try to advance the ball beyond the time line; others try to break players deep as they penetrate the press.

If it is a patterned attack, we have it diagramed quickly. We activate what we consider the best stunt or press against the particular movement.

Whether patterned or free-lance, five attackers in back court can be pressed from baseline to baseline. All our stunts work better where the congregation is larger. The run and jump and the area press were designed to create a chaotic atmosphere against such offensive attacks.

SUMMARY

We divide full court anti-press offenses into three categories: the lane of attack, the method of attack, and the number of attackers. All offenses operate with options from each of these basic categories.

Teams can attack the middle lanes or the side lanes. If they attack the middle lane, they either flash into it or they post a player without much movement within that lane. Or they can combine the two. The first three sections dealt with typical coverage on their avenue of attack.

Primarily, if the opposition wants to go down the side, we force them to the middle; if they want to go down the middle, we fan to the outside. We push them where they do not want to go, where they will have drilled less.

Teams can choose between a short pass method, a long pass approach, a dribble and split maneuver, and a pure patterned assault. The middle five sections displayed our attempts to stop their attacking maneuvers. Again, we tried to force them into unpracticed tactics, thinking they would commit more errors. We even gave an illustration (Virginia Box) of a patterned attack.

Teams can use any number of players in the back court to execute their team attack. Our last five sections dealt with our coverage on the number used. Basically, attackers like to keep the court cleared out for a dribbler against our stunts. But against our team presses, the opposition likes to bring at least three attackers downcourt to bring the ball up the floor: One dribbler could never beat our team presses. We try to keep the attackers guessing by outnumbering them in our stunts, by playing run and jump or area press against a small number, and by employing our stunts against their attacks of three or more. Our team stunts of Chapter 6, our team run and jump press of Chapter 7, and our area man press compel the attackers to bring three or more men into back court. Our stunts make them wish they hadn't.

The defensive tactics we suggested for you to use were just that—suggestions. A defensive coach should ascertain the opponent's mode of attack. He should then decide what he thinks best to destroy that assault. For example, a team might wish to attack with three players, making short passes to cutters in the middle lane. A fan maneuver would force their attack down the outside lanes, making it difficult for them to achieve a good passing angle into the middle lane. The area press with an exaggerated sag would force the long rather than the short pass. And the area press would require the attackers to bring more players into back court to beat the press. Inside the area press are many further adjustments which would force the dribbler-passer to find different passing lanes: for example, 32, 33, 34.

10

Coaching Strategy for Using the Man-to-Man Press

It is important that each coach formulate his preference for defensive play. Before he can make the little decisions that lead to success or failure, the coach must settle on a belief of one defense or a system of defenses. The earlier a coach makes his selection, the longer his time to study and to experiment with his choice.

In this chapter, we intend to show our philosophy and how it leads to our defensive system. We plan on disclosing how we decide on our match-ups, how we plot a blueprint for a game, and how we implement that scheme through our practice schedules. We will describe what we look for during a game which leads to our game adjustments.

PHILOSOPHY

To teach multiple defenses, or to teach one well—that is the question. Each coach must decide for himself whether it is better to stunt from one defense or use a different defense as a change-up.

We believe that one defense learned and executed well will win more games than several defenses learned and executed only adequately. Players quickly spot defensive change-ups, quickly respond to them. Defenders too often get confused at multiple switches.

Besides, we can create a plural look by learning one defense completely. For example, we can play pressure man-to-man. But, during any possession, we can sag and switch on all crosses, making the defense play and look like a match-up zone. All the little things remain constant. For example, the rebounding techniques would be the same. But in teaching multiple defenses, one time down the floor your players may block out individually (man) and the next time they may go down the line of the shot (zone). Defenders who must concentrate on the changing little things will hurt the team defense more than they will help it.

At the full court level, we can manufacture a plural look from only one defense. We can run and jump trap or switch. And from our jump or trap, we can zone pressure the passing lanes; or we can play our assignments man-to-man, leaving only one attacker open if we are in "trap." The possibilities of making our defense appear multiple are endless. And all of it stems from one defense fully covered, completely taught, thoroughly learned.

Teams that use more than one defense too often tell their players that they are inferior, that they must deceive their opposition in order to defeat them. These same teams are never well versed in the basic fundamentals of any one defense. They have to have superior talent to win. And these superior players would have won just as easily with one defense.

Teams that operate from only one defense believe more in themselves and in their defense. They have time to master the fundamental drills of that defense. They learn the little things that win the big games. They develop confidence.

Players do best what they believe will work best. Defenders who are given only one defense believe more quickly in that defense and work harder at performing it better.

We believe in one defense, and we prefer the pressure side of it. It is more advantageous to teach pressure before you start teaching the sags and the stunts. Players respond better from pressure to sag. It is more difficult to get players to react from sag to pressure.

However, during a game, the opposition will function more efficiently during the sagging defensive periods if you go from pressure to sag. So teams that intend to use both for long periods of time should start the game in a slough and extend to pressure.

Stunts must not be taught until the basic defense has been presented and perfected. Stunts tend to weaken the basic defense unless placed in proper perspective. Stunts are used as a change of pace, not as a substitute for the standard defense.

We, too, believe in variety as a change of pace. But our variety comes from stunts out of the same defense: man-to-man. We can change the number of defenders involved from one to the entire team. We can zone the passing lanes or we can jump into man coverage of the passing lanes. We can trap the ball or switch at the point of the ball. Stunts offer innumerable options.

MATCH-UPS

Man-to-man full court presses can oppose their opponents man-to-man by quickness, speed, or height. Each has its advantages.

To match a team by quickness enables the defense to place more pressure on the ball without fear or being beaten by the dribble. To pair speed with speed prevents a breakaway cutter and the ensuing lay-up. Confronting height with height makes for better half-court coverage should the full court pressure prove unsuccessful.

However, the greatest advantage of man-to-man match-ups over zone play lies in the subtle approaches. For example, suppose you have one great defender and the opposition has a skillful ball handler and penetrator. This ball handler must have the ball or the opposition's offense suffers immeasurably. Your adept defender can pressure this ball handler while his teammates operate under the run and no-jump strategy of Chapter 2. Every time the expert driver touches the ball, a defender comes to double-team him. When the proficient penetrator passes the ball, the trapper (not the container) rotates back to his assigned man, or to the open attacker if one of his teammates shot the gap on his original man. The container (the master defender) face-guards the grand ball handler, preventing him from getting the ball back. This is much better strategy than a box-and-one or some zone technique. Again, the little things, such as rebounding, remain constant, allowing complete mastery. And over the long span of a ball game, a season, a career, these little things will prove more effective.

There are many other match-ups that work. Most have been described throughout this book. The inventive coach can match his next opponent's strength against strength and weakness against weakness. Our intentions were to suggest possibilities. It would be impossible to give all the probabilities.

HAVE TWO PLANS

Two plans should be prepared for each opponent: one for the expected and one for the unexpected. Both must be practiced for maximum effectiveness. Both should be fundamentally sound. And both must, by necessity, describe opposite poles. Any adjustment in between the two would not upset the defenders because it would not represent a violent departure.

A new adjustment should always be planned for the second half. Opponents who depend too much upon their coach cannot adequately respond to something new in the second half. And such a coach would only have the one-minute time-outs, instead of the ten minutes at half-time, to adjust his team. Also, each opposing coach should be shown something new the first half. He may waste part of his half-time discussing something he will not see in the second half.

Let's say you have scouted your opponent several times. Each time you scouted them they attacked a man press with a clearout and assaulted a zone press by going down the middle lane with a short passing game. Our basic game plan, therefore, would compel the offense down the outside lanes with the area press. The area press would also eliminate the clearout, and the fan tactics of Chapter 4 would send the ball down the sideline. We would plan on defending the outside lanes with a trap and a jump technique. We would alterate defending the passing lanes with a zone and a man coverage. We would also include certain stunts that would combat our opponent's attack. Our plan might appear as follows:

First Quarter: First two minutes—three men and a tandem.

Second three minutes—fan from run and jump stunts.

Next two minutes—fan from area press, running 33.

Second Quarter: First three minutes—fan from area press, running 34 and 35.

Next five minutes—run containment man from run and jump (center field or left field).

Third Quarter: First four minutes—run face-guard and denial, followed by a run and jump trap.

Last four minutes—run fanning area press from the forty series.

Fourth Quarter: First four minutes—run fanning area press from the twenty series.

Last four minutes—depends upon how game is going.

We open in the three men and a tandem because it would tell us if our scouting reports were accurate and would impel our defenders into motion. We save the last four minutes so that we can adjust according to the score of the game. We certainly would not want to press if we were ahead by 30. We might want extreme pressure if were down by 10.

When we opened in our three men and a tandem, it became obvious that our opponents had developed an excellent outside lane attack, featuring dribbling. We must now alter our game plan. But if we had prepared our defense to compel the offense down the middle, and if we had drilled using zone passing lane principles, our players could easily adjust.

Although our opponents have proved that they can attack down the middle by passing or down the outside by dribbling, we can keep them off-balance with a versatile design. So our game plan would present this look:

First Quarter: First two minutes—three men and a tandem.
Second three minutes—funnel from run
and jump stunts, zoning the passing
lanes.
Next two minutes—fan from area press,
running 34.

Second Quarter: First three minutes—funnel from area
press, running 33 and 35.
Next five minutes—face-guard and denial; once ball is in-bounded, run and
jump switch; man coverage in the passing lanes.

Third Quarter: First four minutes—containment man
defense; no pressure; check their half-
time adjustments.
Next four minutes—run area press (forty
series); alternate from fan to funnel by
our score or no score, unless our opponents decide to run only a middle or an
outside lane attack.

Fourth Quarter: First four minutes—alternate area press
(twenty series) from fan to funnel.
Last four minutes—adjust to the score
and time.

Good teams will quickly defeat a steady diet of any defense.
Today's players adapt too swiftly. That is why zone presses are
not successful for long periods of time. That is why we like to
teach one defense completely.

When you make your game plans, prepare subtle changes
and plenty of them. It is also a good idea to start the second half
with a basic defense. That gives the opposing players time to
forget their half-time instructions.

PRE-SEASON PRACTICES
TO DEVELOP PRESSURE PLAYERS

No coach can effectively teach all the stunts and team defenses described in this book in any one pre-season. Very few

players could learn them all. You must first evaluate your players, unless you can recruit. After objectively evaluating your players, you must decide which stunts and team presses you wish to have for the beginning of the season. List those stunts and presses. Place a date beside each stunt and press. Let that date represent when you plan to introduce that stunt or press.

After the first year, the carry-over value will be a major plus. Each returning player will know everything that was introduced during the previous year. You can also require your coaches in the lower programs to teach all of the material in Chapters 1 through 4.

These fundamentals can be taught in the program below junior high level. But the wise varsity coach will review the fundamentals extensively during each new varsity season. Fundamentals win. That is why these stunts and presses win. They are simply the proper execution of the defensive fundamentals of pressing. Even coaches of the zone presses should require their players to learn and execute the material in Chapters 1 through 4.

As the player graduates to the next phase of the program, he can begin to learn the team techniques of Chapters 6, 7, and 8. When he reaches the varsity level, the player will be completely proficient in all the stunts and team presses.

In pre-season practices, whether in the first year or after several years, the coach must have his players aggressively attack each drill. These players must maintain a positive attitude, which the coach instills subsconsciously by his own approach.

The coach must teach the players the proper mental approach to man-to-man pressure defense; consequently, he can allow no pseudo-pressure. He must immediately remove any player whose stamina is less than adequate. The lack of stamina may only be mental. But a good exercise program on the side of the court will improve the player physically as well as mentally. His next practice will be more impressive.

By repeatedly drilling on the fundamentals, you increase the distance your players can react during the game. Coaches constantly strive to improve their player's jumping and so on. It is equally important to increase their distance of coverage. This is done by repeatedly drilling on pressure drills. Don't teach sag: It will come naturally when you are ready to introduce it.

Fundamentals come first, both in this text and in your practices. Don't be in a hurry to pass up the drills in the first four chapters. They provide enough pressure to get your club through until Christmas; indeed, through the entire season. You can use the holidays to start teaching the run and jump team press and the area man-to-man press. The better your players perform the fundamentals, the better they will execute the team presses. After the first year, you will have your entire pressing system before the first game.

A word of caution: Do not teach the stunts until your half-court and full court fundamentals are mastered. Stunts can hurt the team defense unless they are kept in proper perspective.

PRE-GAME PRACTICES
TO DEVELOP A GAME PLAN

Your opponent's game preparations must change when you do things that they must specifically prepare for. But you should also do the regular things, because it helps your team and it requires other teams to prepare regularly and specifically for you. If you noticed, in the section Have Two Plans, we included regular man defenses, stunts from regular man defenses, and at least two team man defenses. We also primed for the opposite reaction from our opposing coach. Most coaches believe in doing what they have been doing well, but a few will change up on you. So get ready for both.

To prepare for our next week's opponents, we find a quiet corner on the weekend and study our scouting reports on them. We carefully list what we expect them to do. If they want to go down the middle, we force them outside. If they want to dribble, we make them pass. If they want to attack with two excellent dribbler-penetrators, we compel them to use five. In other words, we dictate what we will permit them to do. And then we dominate that dictate.

If we are lucky, both teams will exhibit similar offenses. We try to schedule it that way. But if they represent opposite poles of attacking, it still simplifies our defensive plans. We would prepare for both anyway.

Preparation becomes more difficult when two teams attack with only minor differences. We prime for those minor differences and for their opposites, using four plans. But in the long run, this helps us more by tournament time.

On Monday night we would conclude practice with a two-quarter scrimmage, using our plans for the Tuesday night game. On Thursday we would scrimmage two quarters for our Friday night game. Wednesday and Saturday practices would feature the fundamentals we intend to employ on Tuesday and Friday.

GAME ADJUSTMENTS
TO MAKE PRESS WORK BETTER

"The best laid plans of mice and men go awry." Often, this is true in basketball. More frequently it is not true. But defensive coaches must be prepared for and willing to make game adjustments.

A game adjustment can be as simple as replacing a starter with a substitute. Or, it can be rearranging your personnel to get a quicker or a taller man in a certain spot. Or, it can mean changing the objectives of a certain press. The coach must recognize what is needed and must have the courage to make the change. But he must not act in haste. He must be absolutely sure the adjustment is needed before he acts.

When an effective press can be made even more devastating by a change, the coach must recognize this and make the necessary adjustment. This really takes courage.

Some defenses are self-adjusting. The area man-to-man press, for instance, can be adjusted to have a gap shooter on any passing lane (see Chapter 8).

Other adjustments can be made to strengthen the defense for that one game. Let's say that the offense has been driving around the taller, slower front line defenders of the area press. By placing the quicker back line players up front, the defense could stop the dribble penetration, forcing the pass. Once the passing attack begins to take its toll, the defensive coach can adjust by putting the taller players back up front. These taller players would not only encourage the dribble, but they could deflect low two-handed overhead passes.

Experience teaches the coach when to make adjustments and what type will be best. Too many intangibles render it impossible to formulate set rules. Frequently, we will experiment during the first half. Then, during the second half, we will employ the best of the tests.

Where we discussed a defense or a stunt, we explained what it forced the opposer to do. We also stated what that defense or stunt worked best against and what gave it trouble. A coach must learn these pros and cons if he is to make the best game adjustments possible.

GAME-TO-GAME ADJUSTMENTS

Your defense must be flexible enough to allow game-to-game adjustments. Man-to-man presses enjoy such resiliency.

The opponents we face on Tuesday night might prefer a passing attack. The opponents on Friday night might like the dribble invasion. Therefore, on Tuesday night we would place our big men up front in the area press, while on Friday night we would have our quick men manning the front stations. This would encourage our Tuesday foe to dribble and our Friday adversary to pass.

COACHES MUST ALSO ANALYZE AND REACT

Just as coaches hope their players will analyze the opposition's attack and react in a way favorable to the defense, players expect their coaches to analyze and react as well. It takes knowledge, experience, foresight, and courage. This book can give you knowledge. Time can render experience. Experience gives you foresight. But only you can give yourself courage.

The defensive coach has many opportunities to analyze his defense. He may find the need for adjustments in his early practice sessions. When he prepares for a game, he may find that a particular strategy will not work. Perhaps it does not work because of the placement of personnel. Perhaps faulty logic has been used. While playing the game, a coach may see the need for a change. A substitute might be all that is needed. But the greatest opportunity to analyze and react comes at the end of the season. At that time, the coach can keep a cool head, study the data properly, and adjust his defense according to his findings. He can create an addition. Or he can start from a different point and bring about a new approach. But he must remember: Unless his new approach coincides with his personality, he will never successfully teach it.

In your hands, coach, rests the decision of which press or which stunt to use. Gather all the facts and make the best judgment possible. It's lonely at the head of the bench.

Index

DATE DUE

MAR 29 '79		
OCT 9 '79		
NO 3 '82		
DEC 1 5 1983		
JUN 6 1988		
MY 14 '90		
DE 17 '91		